Accelerated Quantum Technologies Change Management

Accelerated Quantum Technologies Change Management

Gregory J. Skulmoski, PhD

BEP

BUSINESS EXPERT PRESS

Leader in applied, concise business books

Accelerated Quantum Technologies Change Management

First published in 2025 by
Business Expert Press, LLC
222 East 46th Street, New York, NY 10017
www.businessexpertpress.com

ISBN-13: 978-1-63742-908-2 (paperback)
ISBN-13: 978-1-63742-909-9 (e-book)

Portfolio and Project Management Collection

First edition: 2025

10 9 8 7 6 5 4 3 2 1

EU SAFETY REPRESENTATIVE
Mare Nostrum Group B.V.
Mauritskade 21D
1091 GC Amsterdam
The Netherlands
gpsr@mare-nostrum.co.uk

Description

Accelerated Quantum Technologies Change Management offers business and technology leaders a practical guide to navigating and accelerating their organization's quantum technology journey.

Quantum technologies are rapidly emerging across digital ecosystems with transformative potential—from breakthroughs in pharmaceuticals and climate modeling to risks that threaten current cybersecurity standards. While these technologies present remarkable opportunities, they also pose urgent challenges, particularly the threat of quantum-enabled attacks on classical encryption systems. There is Q-Day and Encryptogeddon to navigate.

Despite the growing importance of quantum readiness, many organizations face significant adoption barriers, including a lack of internal capabilities and general uncertainty about where to begin. This book addresses those challenges with precision.

Greg Skulmoski presents a structured, front-end change management approach to help organizations overcome "quantum hesitancy" and to accelerate adoption. He tailors widely accepted change management practices to build awareness, inspire desire, and develop the knowledge necessary to plan, implement, and optimize quantum solutions.

Drawing on lessons from ultrafast construction projects—such as the 12-day delivery of an 1,800-bed field hospital in Wuhan, China—Skulmoski explores how schedule compression techniques can be applied to quantum technology projects. Leaders are guided through a practical evaluation of these advanced techniques to align with organizational risk tolerance and quantum technology strategic goals.

Written for quantum champions, IT and cybersecurity leaders, project managers, digital executives, and board members, this book equips decision makers with the strategic insight and tactical tools needed to confidently lead quantum technology change management projects—turning uncertainty into opportunity.

Contents

List of Figures and Tables

Figures

List of Tables

Review Quotes

"A compelling narrative"

"The case study of the Wuhan hospitals, used to demonstrate the concept of schedule compression, is both captivating and effective. By drawing parallels between the urgency and precision required to build hospitals during a crisis and the need to accelerate quantum adoption under looming cybersecurity threats, the book successfully turns abstract project management concepts into a compelling narrative. For organizations that feel behind or unsure where to start, this book provides not only a place to begin but a strategy to move forward with coherence and purpose".—**Samuel Tseitkin, CEO, ExeQuantum, Australia**

"A must-read for project managers, IT security leaders, and business executives"

"Overall, Accelerated Quantum Technologies Change Management *is excellent and the use of the Prosci ADKAR model for change management is a significant strength. It provides a structured approach to organizational change, which is crucial when adopting new technologies like quantum computing.*

This book is a must-read for project managers, IT security leaders, and business executives seeking to accelerate their organization's integration of quantum technologies. It offers a straightforward approach to change management and strategic planning, making it an indispensable resource for navigating the complexities associated with implementing quantum technology solutions."
—**Nick Gibbons, Cofounder, BlockLock, UK**

"A rare resource…not only useful but also visionary"

"Accelerated Quantum *provides a robust foundation for any organization looking to prepare for the quantum era. By integrating familiar frameworks such as the PMBOK Guide, Information Technology Infrastructure Library (ITIL) Service Management, and the NIST Cybersecurity Framework, Dr. Greg Skulmoski connects quantum readiness with established best practices. This strategic alignment helps demystify quantum technologies and embeds them within an actionable roadmap. Whether you're in the C-suite, on the board, or leading digital transformations, the book offers a clear and credible pathway to incorporate quantum into your organization's future planning—without requiring a PhD in physics or deep technical background in cryptography.*

What makes this book especially valuable is its practicality. The inclusion of diagnostic tools—like the Quantum Barriers to Adoption Gizmo—offers readers immediate ways to evaluate readiness and take action. Concepts such as 100-day plans and schedule compression are clearly explained through real-world examples, making it easy for business leaders to apply the guidance in meaningful ways. As someone from the financial industry who transitioned into quantum without a technical background, I found this book both empowering and accessible. It's a rare resource that informs without overwhelming. As I often say, and as Greg emphasizes throughout: "Start getting ready NOW because quantum is coming and it's not a question of if—it's only about when." This book is not only useful but also visionary."—**Bob Dameron, Consultant, HorizonX Consulting, North America**

"Expert insight into quantum technologies project scheduling"

"*Greg's expert insight into quantum technologies project scheduling to consider schedule compression early, during strategy formulation is precisely a best practice. His clear presentation of advanced concepts like the balance between crashing and fast tracking and risk management makes these complex methods accessible and strategically actionable. By introducing these techniques up front, Greg equips readers to anticipate and manage risks before they escalate. His explanation of the technical maturity stack is groundbreaking.* Accelerated Quantum Technologies Change Management *is the resource for insightful schedule management and is an essential resource for profession-als in high-stakes project environments."*—**Alan Patching, PhD, Former CEO of Stadium Australia Trust (Owning Entity of the Sydney Olym-pic Stadium, Australia)**

"Navigate the complex and rapidly evolving world of quantum"

"Executives seeking clarity in the face of quantum disruption will find Ac-celerated Quantum Technologies Change Management both timely and empowering. This book stands out by transforming a highly technical subject into a user-focused, actionable guide—offering "a comprehensive framework for organizational change and technology adoption." Rather than isolating quantum as a purely technical challenge, it integrates a structured change management and adoption framework with well-established program and project management practices. The result? A holistic roadmap that shows you not just how to understand quantum, but how to embed it into your strategic agenda.

This is not a theoretical or academic exercise—it's a practical playbook to navigate the complex and rapidly evolving world of quantum. Executives will especially value the clever diagnostic "Gizmos" that help assess readiness and cut through complexity, along with targeted change models and practical 100-day plans designed for real-world implementation. These tools translate strategy into action, helping leaders overcome barriers and accelerate timelines with confidence. As the book reminds us, this is a resource that is as useful as it is visionary. For those preparing their organizations to lead in the quan-tum era, this book is essential reading."—**Thomas Matheus, PhD, CTO, Cystel, UK**

"Intersection of quantum technology and organizational change"

"Accelerated Quantum Technologies Change Management *fills a critical gap by addressing the intersection of quantum technology and organizational change—an area that few resources tackle with the same level of intention and structure. By combining established industry frameworks such as ADKAR, PMBOK Guide, ITIL, NIST CSF, and Mosca's Theorem, the book builds on a reliable structure while adapting these methodologies specifically for the quantum context. This approach ensures executives and leaders not only understand the technology but also have a strategic, structured way to implement it within their organizations.*

What truly sets this book apart is its practicality and urgency. The "Start Now Imperative" and 100-day plan provide readers with more than just theory— they offer actionable steps to address the quantum transformation challenge immediately. Through visual tools, maturity models, gap analyses, and adoption determinant tables, the book becomes an invaluable resource for executives, PMOs, and cybersecurity professionals alike. It goes beyond technology, addressing human resistance, leadership buy-in, stakeholder engagement, and ensuring sustained organizational readiness. This is the guide you need to lead with confidence in the rapidly evolving quantum era."—**Julio Bandeira de Melo (LLB, CISM, CRISC, CISA, CCSK, ECIH, CCT, CC), Senior Cybersecurity Leader, Resources Industry Leader, Chair of EC-Council Scheme Committee, Author, Peer Reviewer, Calgary, Canada**

"Real-world case studies add depth and relevance"

"*Accelerated Quantum Technologies Change Management is a thought-provoking and timely contribution to the emerging discourse on quantum technology adoption. The book offers a nuanced and practical lens on how organizations can approach the shift to quantum—balancing strategic ambitions with cybersecurity imperatives. In a landscape where quantum is moving from theoretical promise to practical services, this work provides a well-structured framework for managing change in a field still largely undefined. The author's insights into stakeholder engagement, agile methodologies, and the distinction between strategic innovation and security-driven initiatives are especially relevant as quantum adoption begins to echo the recent surge in AI initiatives. Including real-world case studies (the Wuhan hospital project) adds depth and relevance, drawing parallels between established project challenges and those emerging in quantum programs. A must-read for leaders navigating the complex road to quantum readiness.*"—**Andrew Beer, Programme Director, Microsoft, Qatar**

"A highly practical and timely guide"

"Accelerated Quantum *is a highly practical and timely guide that bridges the critical gap between quantum technology's potential and organizational readiness. Grounded in well-established change management frameworks familiar to project teams, it is set to equip business leaders, project managers, and cybersecurity executives with the strategic and tactical tools needed to accelerate the adoption of quantum technologies".*—**Steve Vaile, Consulting Director of Quantum Security Defence**

"A compelling and thought-provoking companion"

"Accelerated Quantum *bridges the gap between vision and execution in the quantum era through a strategy-first, standards-driven approach that is key to successfully managing adoption barriers. Greg Skulmoski empowers quantum champions to turn bold quantum ambitions into real-world outcomes by aligning strategy with implementation. The book has proven to be a compelling and thought-provoking companion in my exploration of quantum topics—perfect for self-directed learning. It offers clear, practical guidance that I can use when I speak about quantum technologies adoption in support of my book Quantum Nation: India's Leap into the Future."*—**L. Venkata Subramaniam, PhD (Indian Institute of Technology Delhi, India), IBM Quantum India Lead, IBM Master Inventor**

"Presents a clear roadmap for quantum readiness"

"Accelerated Quantum *is a timely and practical guide that empowers organizations to navigate the coming era of quantum technologies. Gregory Skulmoski reframes quantum disruption from an abstract concern into a structured, actionable transformation agenda. Balancing the promise of quantum innovation with urgent cybersecurity risks posed by cryptographically-relevant quantum computers, the book offers a dual-strategy approach: harnessing quantum opportunities while securing systems with post-quantum cryptography.*

Grounded in industry standards such as ITIL, ISO 31000, and the PMBOK Guide, Accelerated Quantum *presents a clear roadmap for quantum readiness. Its accessible tone breaks through technical inertia and speaks directly to professionals across IT, cybersecurity, strategy, and innovation. Standout chapters on schedule compression draw on compelling examples—such as the rapid Wuhan hospital build—to illustrate fast tracking, crashing, and associated risk.*

The book's disciplined yet flexible strategies empower leaders to "just start" and overcome analysis paralysis. Accelerated Quantum *by Gregory Skulmoski is more than a guide—it's a blueprint for thriving in the quantum era.".*
—Muria Roberts, Founder and Chair of Tasmanian Quantum Network, Director of QTM-X

Author's Note

In this book, we[1] have conducted a peer review to collect feedback to find and fix any errors, identify gaps, and to clarify ambiguous concepts. We have developed a heterogeneous sample of subject matter experts from (i) project and program management, (ii) quantum technology service providers, and (iii) business leadership. We have used purposive and snowball techniques to find our subject matter experts and to address any reliability, validity, and bias risks. We have provided *Accelerated Quantum Technologies Change Management* to 14 people, and 11 returned constructive feedback that we gratefully accepted and incorporated into this book. For example, we have revised a few sentences for clarity and added additional content and figures to strengthen the main points. Thank you. Our expert reviewers also provided positive praise, which we share with you.

---

[1]In this book, I—the author, Greg Skulmoski—use the "editorial we" to refer only to myself and previous authors I have collaborated with in this book series. "We" does not include the reader, previous employers, past employers, and so on. "We" includes only Dr. Ashkan Memari and I, who wrote *Quantum Cybersecurity Program Management*, and Chris Walker and I, who wrote *Cybersecurity Training: A Pathway to Readiness*. I include my coauthors because their contributions and influences are carried forward in this book. For this reason, I avoid using "I" and use "we" despite contradicting the American Psychological Association's first-person pronoun advice that if the manuscript is written by myself, then the author should use the pronoun "I" to refer to oneself. Instead, I use the "editorial we" to also say thank-you to my coauthors.

Preface

Perhaps the "sudden" interest in quantum technologies was amplified by the United Nations declaring 2025 the International Year of Quantum Science and Technology and a steady stream of content from respected quantum technologies experts advising organizations to start their quantum journeys without delay. Some organizations have delayed their quantum technology projects because their focus was on near-term projects (e.g., implementing AI and zero trust technologies or complying with emerging regulations). The result is some organizations wish to "catch up" in a hurry but may not have a clear plan or know where to start. Indeed, there may be barriers to adoption within the organization that first need to be managed.

Accelerated Quantum Technologies Change Management was written to provide a framework for organizations and individuals to quickly begin their quantum journey. We structured the book to scaffold learning beginning with an introduction to the basics of quantum technologies and change management. This provides a foundation to develop the critical quantum strategy—business, technology, and cybersecurity—followed by a program of quantum technology projects. Should the strategy be weak or misaligned, project teams will likely struggle to successfully deliver change. However, some organizations face barriers to adopting quantum technologies; these barriers need to be addressed to strategize, plan, implement and optimize quantum technologies. To break through adoption barriers, we review technology adoption best practices suitable for quantum technologies. Some organizations may wish to accelerate their quantum technologies program using schedule compression methods. We review schedule compression theory and best practices including the Leishenshan Hospital project in Wuhan, China where a COVID-19 field hospital was built in 12 days to provide an 1800-bed facility using fast tracking, crashing and substituting methods. We bring all these change management elements together to structure an accelerated plan to break through any quantum barriers and to begin the organization's quantum journey. We also outline a 100-day plan followed by concluding thoughts.

This book is unique by taking a change management approach aligned with standards and frameworks to guide organizations through the front-end of the quantum journey that may include quantum technologies adoption barriers and delayed strategy development. This is not a quantum technology book that surveys the latest technology because as soon as the book is published, no doubt these technologies will be outdated or even obsolete. Look elsewhere for more up-to-date information about emerging quantum technologies.

Organizations wishing for an accelerated pathway to quantum technologies may consider schedule compression as a tactic; however, fast tracking and crashing are complex and risky techniques that need careful review to determine their appropriateness.

Accelerated Quantum may be appealing to at least three distinct groups of stakeholders:

1. **Business leaders:** The business leader (e.g., board members, C-suite, executives, and department directors and managers) responsible for the organization's digital products and/or services will learn how to accelerate the front-end of change management to progress their quantum journey and how to strategize for risky compressed schedule projects.
2. **IT security leadership:** The IT security leadership team and subject matter experts will appreciate the actionable plans aligned with leading change management frameworks to break through quantum cybersecurity barriers.
3. **Quantum champions:** The quantum champions throughout the organization will better comprehend the complexities of a quantum technologies change management program involving cybersecurity, business use cases, and a quantum infrastructure. They will also learn strategies to develop sustained funding and leadership support.

With this book in your hand, it is evidence you truly are a quantum champion. Amazing, only a few years ago, neither of us were on this quantum journey.

What Is Microlearning?

There are many ways to learn, like reviewing the glossary in this book. Traditional learning typically involves attending a course for a day or two, but retention fades over time unless the new learnings are applied or refreshed. Microlearning, on the other hand, allows learners to gain practical knowledge incrementally. It becomes more effective when paired with a learning to-do list and engagement with online topics of interest. This approach fosters ongoing learning through extended learning opportunities to support a sustainable career. Explore topics from this book online to deepen your understanding.

Microlearning

We invite you to search[2] online and use other technologies to find additional information about topics of interest. You may set up alerts to receive content covered in this book:

- Review best practices for generating or finding information online like using Boolean searches and generative AI prompts;
- Track your industry and discipline's quantum technologies transformation trends, business use case implications and opportunities;
- Become familiar with quantum privacy and cybersecurity-related regulations in your industry including any international, national, and local jurisdictions.

---

[2]We use the term "search online" broadly to mean using online resources and generative artificial intelligence to learn more about topics in Microlearning sections. For example, we refer the reader to search for templates rather than direct them to a specific website because each reader has unique needs and interests.

Foreword

"A consequential conversation with humility and clarity"
By John Keith King

Former White House Lead Communications Engineer, U.S. Department of State, and Joint Chiefs of Staff in the Pentagon. Veteran U.S. Navy, Top Secret/SCI Security Clearance.

Quantum is not a topic for the faint of heart. It challenges our assumptions about computation, upends traditional models of cybersecurity, and demands that we rethink how digital systems are built, protected, and evolved. *Accelerated Quantum* meets that challenge head-on—and delivers a roadmap that is as technically grounded as it is organizationally astute.

Greg Skulmoski has crafted a highly valuable and timely guide for quantum champions, CISOs (chief information security officers), enterprise architects, and transformation leaders who recognize that quantum readiness is no longer optional. The convergence of post-quantum cryptography mandates, accelerated quantum research breakthroughs, and real-world risk from nation-state adversaries makes the urgency palpable. This book doesn't just argue for immediate action—it shows you how to begin, structure, and lead with precision.

What I found especially compelling is the pragmatic scaffolding built into every chapter. From the application of Mosca's Theorem in prioritizing cryptographic migrations, to schedule compression strategies drawn from real-world crisis scenarios to technical maturity assessment "Gizmos" that elevate internal decision making—Greg has clearly lived at the intersection of theory and execution. His integration of ADKAR, NIST, ITIL, and project portfolio best practices will resonate with any organization seeking to embed quantum into their broader digital risk and innovation agenda.

Just as importantly, the writing respects its readers. It doesn't oversimplify or pander—it invites intelligent professionals into a complex, consequential conversation with humility and clarity.

In my career, I've been privileged to help lead secure communications for the highest levels of U.S. government, and I've rarely seen a field evolve as quickly—or with stakes as high—as quantum cybersecurity. This book is a rare contribution: part blueprint, part warning flare, and part call to arms.

If you're holding this book, you're likely among those entrusted to shape your organization's digital future. Read on—and get started. There's no time to waste.

Acknowledgments

When you write a book, you recall and appreciate the many people who have helped you along the way. This is my fourth book and the guidance I received for my first book from amazing reviewers like Irene Corpuz has been carried forward. The list of people to thank is long and I am fortunate to have many people guide me throughout my career and education. I am grateful to the professors whose red ink overwhelmed my black type which helped me reflect and learn. We thank the many peer reviewers who gave up their evenings and weekends to diligently comment and provide constructive feedback.

The Business Expert Press team were extremely helpful and supportive, including Dr. Kam Jugdev, Charlene Kronstedt, and Scott Isenberg. The editorial team at S4 Carlisle helped improve the quality of the text. The team members and inspiring leaders in past projects at Regina Qu'Appelle Health Region (project finance), Stream Data Systems (Y2K mitigation projects), and Cleveland Clinic Abu Dhabi (complex and emerging medical technologies) showed me how to apply project and change management theories in a lean and practical approach.

I am grateful to have worked on multiple Project Management Institute standards projects that opened my eyes and heart to best practices. John Schlichter led our Organizational Project Management Maturity Model project and Cindy Berg led the 2000 PMBOK Guide update—great leaders both of you! Finally, my family and friends who have encouraged me along my dual career paths: project manager and academic. Thank you kindly.

CHAPTER 1

Introduction

> *It's not about how late you start; it's about how well you finish.*
>
> Unknown

My dad could fix and build just about anything. He used to say "measure twice, cut once" which has stuck with me throughout my career. In this book, despite the goal of an accelerated start to quantum technology project, it is prudent to plan to reduce implementation risks, waste, and rework. The ideal quantum journey might have or should have started many years ago; however, the quantum journey will be more predictable with a comprehensive approach to guide change and project planning despite pressures to quickly plan, implement, and optimize quantum computing.

The Quantum Journey

There is increased reporting about quantum computing threats and benefits that represent the dual potentialities of technology; it can be used for both negative and positive purposes. Robert Iger wrote "innovate or die" and organizations now are adopting quantum computing and protecting their data and systems from quantum cyberattacks. Organizations are advised to conduct a gap analysis of their current and target state capabilities (also known as the future state) and update their strategies to adopt quantum technologies. Then, develop, prioritize, and initiate quantum technology use cases to bring the organization progressively closer to their quantum goals. These quantum technology use cases will be for business innovation and cybersecurity projects like post-quantum cryptographic[3]

---

[3]Post-quantum cryptography is a classically implemented defensive strategy meant to counteract quantum threats, specifically quantum computers capable

migrations and cryptographic agility (the ability to update the organization's cryptography efficiently and effectively). To gauge the size of this organizational effort, it could take 10 to 20 years to fully protect the organization's systems and data with new cryptography based on previous cryptographic migrations (NIST 2024b, 8).

However, many organizations face barriers to initiating quantum technology projects and adopting quantum computing such as a lagging regulatory environment. We review barriers to adoption and change management strategies and approaches to break through any quantum barriers.

Some organizations are early in their quantum journeys and may also wish to speed up with project schedule compression strategies and tactics like crashing and fast tracking to gain market share. These advanced scheduling techniques were used to great success during the initial 2020 COVID-19 (coronavirus disease 2019) pandemic to quickly build two hospitals in Wuhan, China, to address escalating healthcare needs. For example, the 1,800-bed Leishenshan hospital was built in just 12 days! We detail and apply their schedule compression best practices to quantum technology projects. However, these schedule compression techniques are inherently risky and should be used with caution to avoid waste and rework on quantum technology projects. We guide the reader through a risk management approach[4] to analyze the feasibility of using schedule compression on their quantum technology project with tactics to improve the probability of schedule compression success.

Quantum Journey Context

The context for this book is understood by asking, "Where do I start with quantum technologies to catch up?" These technologies follow the typical

---

of breaking existing encryption. Post-quantum cryptography are cryptographic methods designed to protect against cyber-attacks by cryptographically-relevant quantum and classical computers. Therefore, post-quantum cryptography is a classical technology and not a quantum technology.

[4]When we write about risks, we also include issues. For example, the risk register also includes an issue register but is referred to as the risk register for brevity. Therefore, for conciseness, we avoid "risks and issues" and instead write only "risks."

End Users of Quantum Technologies

Pre-Project	Project	Post-Project
Quantum Project Sponsor	Project Manager	Project Sponsor Business Case Owner

Demand leading up through **Quantum Business Case** ← **Quantum Project** → **Quantum Project Deliverables** → **Value**

Continual Improvement

| | | Growth | Maturity | Decline |

ADKar   adk**A**r   adka**R**

ADKAR Change Management

awareness, desire, knowledge, ability and reinforcement

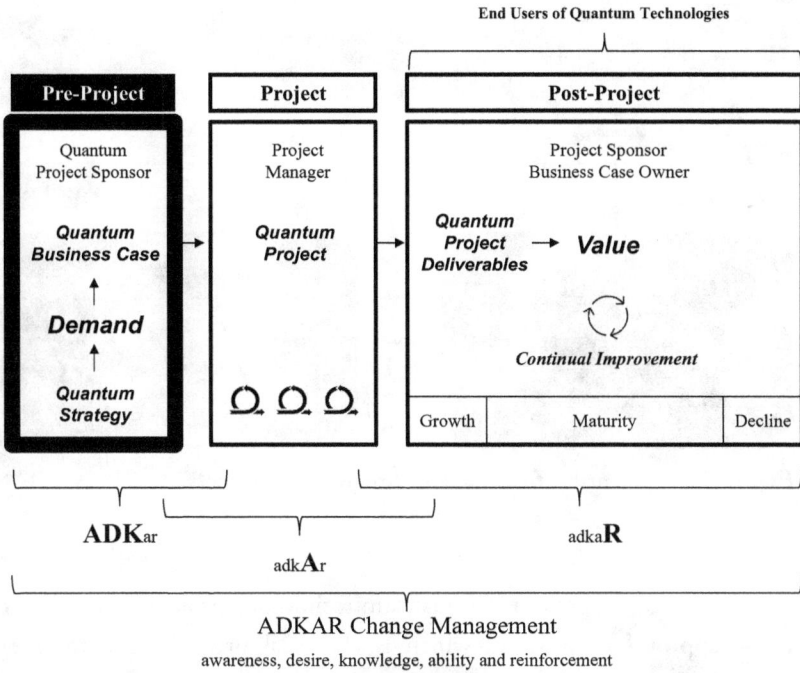

Figure 1.1 Quantum technologies life cycle

technologies life cycle (Figure 1.1). The life cycle begins with a pre-project phase, followed by projects to implement technologies, then the technologies are used by their intended users in the post-project phase. There are growth, maturity, and decline phases where technologies are decommissioned. This book is about the pre-project phase to develop awareness, desire, and knowledge of the program of quantum technology projects and to provide a framework to accelerate the organization's quantum journey, especially if there are barriers to adoption. We recommend reviewing and developing quantum technology strategies in the pre-project phase.

The quantum technologies life cycle begins with an idea of how to use quantum technologies to advance the goals of the organization. That inspiration is elaborated into a business case and proposed for approval during a capital and operational expenditure (CapEx/OpEx) budgeting cycle. If approved and funded, organizations initiate a program of quantum technology projects to close technology gaps (Figure 1.2) and the focus of a previous book: *Quantum Cybersecurity Program Management* (Skulmoski and Memari 2025a).

Current State	Target State
Gaps and Opportunities Identified *Demand*	Improved Cybersecurity Readiness and Quantum Capabilities *Value*

Technical Maturity Optimization Projects

1. Project Management
2. Service Management
3. Change Management
4. Cybersecurity Management

Quantum Projects

1. Cybersecurity Foundation
2. Quantum Awareness
3. Cryptographic Agility
4. Quantum Technologies Implementation
5. Post-Quantum Cryptographic Migrations

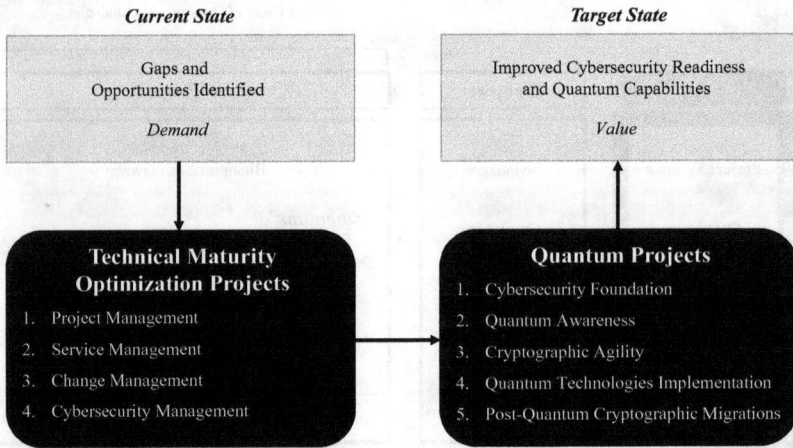

Figure 1.2 Quantum technologies program of projects

To initiate the program of quantum technology projects, there needs to be approval to proceed, which is a critical pre-project state gate. The pre-project phase is also the beginning of organizational change management.

Organizational Change Management

In this book, we introduce organizational change management[5] to improve the probability of accelerating the front-end of the quantum computing program. Implementing a program of quantum computing projects is out of scope for this book.

Organizational change management research and practice has a long history. The Prosci ADKAR model[6] is a popular change management approach and includes five steps also known as milestones. First,

---

[5]Project change management occurs within project boundaries, while organizational change management spans before, during, and after the project to ensure the intended value is realized in business operations.

[6]When ADKAR is entirely capitalized, we use the term to refer to the entire change management process including the front-end, the project, and post-project. Capitalization helps to identify the change management phase (e.g., the desire phase is written as aDkar).

to create change, build *awareness*, *desire*, and *knowledge* in change management stakeholders (ADKar) for quantum technologies. Then provide the change (adkAr) or the *ability* (e.g., the project deliverables through a project delivery approach). Finally, *reinforcement* of the change (adkaR) where quantum computing adoption is managed and scaled according to the strategies outlined in the original quantum computing business case. The ADKAR approach has been widely used in technology adoption projects (Parlakkiliç and Ünalan 2021; Da Veiga 2018).

The ADKAR approach also helps to distinguish the three main phases of technology service management (Figure 1.1). There is a technology service management planning and strategy development phase, followed by a project that provides valued deliverables that are handed over to IT operations. Then in the post-project phase, IT operations manage the technology used to provide the intended value outlined in the business case. Indeed, the pre-project, project, and post-project (operational) phases align precisely with the project boundaries illustrated in the PMBOK Guide standard (Project Management Institute 2017a, 562). Therefore, the change management, technology service management and project management phases can be overlapped and aligned.

The many organizational change management standards and frameworks offer similar insights that can guide quantum technologies change management. The Prosci ADKAR model provides an overall framework that is grouped into three phases. The Association of Change Management Professionals (2025) *Standard for Change Management* provides additional content that is generally accepted and applicable to most change management projects like adopting quantum technologies. The PMBOK Guide standard supports project teams. Finally, the Information Technology Infrastructure Library (ITIL) Service Management framework supports the change management process as it is technology oriented and therefore suited to quantum technologies. Together, these standards and frameworks are applied, combined, and tailored for *Accelerated Quantum Technologies Change Management*.

In our approach (Figure 1.2) there is a *current state* or pre-project state, and a *target state* made possible through projects and their deliverables that provide value to end users. Moving from a current to a target state is common to change management models and is also the foundation of business frameworks and standards like the *Cybersecurity Framework* (NIST 2024a), the ITIL (AXELOS 2019) *Service Management Framework*, and program management in *The Standard for Program Management* (Project Management Institute 2017b).

To bring this introduction to its end, *Accelerated Quantum Technologies Change Management* aligns with generally accepted standards and frameworks with the goal of helping quantum champions progress through the front-end of their quantum journey. The change management approach in this book is tailored based on multiple approaches including Prosci change management which will be appreciated by certified ADKAR practitioners. It is not the Prosci ADKAR Model that is of central importance in this book but rather combining and tailoring change management with technology management best practices[7] that are tuned for quantum computing when a swift completion is the program priority. This is not a one-size-fits-all book; rather, it is a place to start your quantum journey and then tailor to your unique organization.

Organizations and its people are increasingly enthused with quantum technologies and are joining the quantum journey whether it be an organizational or personal journey. Quantum technologies bring great promise and risks that some have called *Encryptogeddon*. Before detailing a strategic and risk management approach to quantum technologies adoption, first we give a brief overview of quantum technologies in the next chapter.

---

[7]In this book, the term *best practices* refers to business practices that lead to superior results. The best practices in this book are generally applicable and apply to most projects, most of the time. For best practices to appear in international standards (e.g., the PMBOK Guide) and frameworks (e.g., the NIST Cybersecurity Framework), they often must prove themselves to be generally accepted as best practices which can take many years. *Leading practices*, according to John Schlichter are like best practices but are new and used by early adopters. With time, leading practices may become generally accepted (rather than a fad) and may work themselves into standards and frameworks. While some may distinguish between best and leading practices, we do not. Instead, best practices may include leading practices in this book.

Microlearning

Change management is a well-studied topic with many resources on-line. Learn about:

- Change management case studies in your industry for implementation ideas,
- Change management approaches that are used in your organization,
- The gap analysis approach is regularly used in projects and strategy development: look for quantum technologies-specific approaches.
- How are other organizations in your industry preparing for Encryptogeddon?

CHAPTER 2

Quantum Technology Basics

The expert in anything was once a beginner.

Helen Hayes

Albert Einstein was perplexed by quantum phenomena which he wrote was "spooky action at a distance."[8] While the complexity of quantum mechanics was a bit beyond Einstein, today that complexity is managed by subject matter experts (SMEs), like quantum business analysts, project managers, electrical engineers, and algorithm developers. However, understanding the basics of quantum technologies gives the reader insight into these new technology projects. Appreciating the basics fosters awareness, desire, and knowledge for the program of quantum computing.

Quantum Technologies 101

Quantum technologies (the behavior of matter and energy) is a subset of digital technologies and is often described in terms of quantum mechanics, a mathematical representation of subatomic particles. Since quantum mechanics is a *different* way of mathematics, quantum technologies process data differently than classical computers resulting in many computational advantages. There are three major categories of quantum technologies, namely, quantum sensors, quantum communications, and quantum computing.

---

[8]Albert Einstein wrote to Max Born in 1947 about quantum mechanics and the translation from German is "physics should represent a reality in time and space, free from spooky action at a distance" (*spukhafte fernwirkung*). In *The Born-Einstein letters: correspondence between Albert Einstein and Max and Hedwig Born from 1916–1955, with commentaries by Max Born*. Macmillan, 1971, 158.

1. **Quantum sensors** can provide unrivaled precision and sensitivity with far-reaching applications like measuring minuscule changes in the earth's crust to forecast a significant geological event such as an earthquake, enhancing mining exploration and safety, and improving weather forecasting. Quantum sensors also promise improved healthcare diagnostics.

2. **Quantum communications** also known as the "quantum internet" provides improved communications performance. Rather than using mathematics as the basis for encryption, quantum key distribution (QKD) uses the properties of light (photons) to provide encryption and decryption capabilities. The quantum internet is predicted to improve the performance of other quantum technologies including quantum sensing and computing.

3. **Quantum computers** differ from classical computers in their architecture and how they process data. While classical computing is based on bits, quantum computing is based on qubits, the smallest unit of data. A principal difference between bits and qubits is classical computers process data sequentially, while a quantum computer can process data concurrently. That is, a bit can either be a one or a zero; however, a qubit can be both like 65 percent zero and 35 percent one. The result is quantum computers appear "faster"[9] because quantum mathematics is different from the classical computing binary approach. Increasing the bit size in classical super computers increases its power linearly while increasing qubits increases computing power exponentially. Quantum computing was first proposed by Richard Feynman (1982) who previously won the Nobel Prize in Physics and led the way for future quantum researchers like Peter Shor, Lov Grover, Michele Mosca, Darío Gil, and L. Venkata Subramaniam.

Therefore, quantum computing is generally appealing due to the hyper speed of some computations. Quantum computers are built for special

---

[9]Due to concurrent calculations with a quantum computer, to find the optimal result fewer steps of calculations are required resulting in finishing sooner than a classical computer rather than being *faster*.

purposes like searching or optimization rather than an all-purpose computer like the laptop computer. The benefits (and threats) of quantum computing, including improved performance, can be explained by quantum parallelism, superposition, and entanglement ("spooky action at a distance"), and we leave it to the reader to further explore these concepts.

Building quantum computers is complex because the quantum phenomena is fragile; the surrounding environment reduces the quantum effect in a process known as decoherence. Fault-tolerant technologies are emerging to reduce the effects of decoherence—inaccurate and unreliable computations. The effective interplay between decoherence and fault tolerance is a determining factor to scale up enough qubits so a quantum computer can outperform a classical computer (e.g., the quantum advantage milestone[10]).

Decoherence, scaling, quantum parallelism, superposition, and entanglement can be overwhelming, but remember, this is quantum physics terminology; you and I are users of these technologies rather than design engineers and physics researchers. Luckily, we can simplify quantum technologies (including quantum computing) into hardware, software, and integration. Computer hardware does little by itself and is paired with software like quantum algorithms to provide value to the user. The final component is the integration of quantum technologies with the broader digital ecosystem where quantum and classical computing (including high performance computing) are used sequentially and concurrently in a hybrid digital environment. When viewed as hardware, software, and integration, quantum technologies change and project management becomes less mysterious.

Quantum Algorithms

To plan, implement, and optimize quantum software applications, apply the ITIL technology management framework[11]. There are two main types

---

[10]Quantum advantage is used rather than quantum supremacy that may have racist overtones for some.

[11]COBIT (Control Objectives for Information and Related Technologies) is another technology management framework that can also be used in conjunction with this book rather than ITIL Service Management.

of quantum algorithms: custom developed and off-the-shelf. Custom algorithms are planned, developed, tested, and implemented in a similar way to software engineering (e.g., DevOps). The off-the-shelf quantum software applies algorithms to business workflows and are provided by major technology companies like SAP's early chemistry workflows that leverage quantum technologies. Chemists follow commonly used SAP chemistry workflows that are supported with classical technologies where some steps in the process will receive a performance boost with quantum computing in the cloud. Off-the-shelf quantum algorithm projects can be planned, implemented, and optimized with standard project management tools (e.g., work breakdown structures [WBSs] and schedules) and processes (e.g., project planning) and ITIL practices (e.g., Service Validation and Testing practice).

Quantum algorithms are used to solve problems (e.g., searching, optimizing, or simulating). The most famous are Shor's and Grover's quantum algorithms. Quantum algorithms are powered by quantum computers with a quantum processor (hardware). Organizations are migrating to quantum-resistant algorithms to protect their data and systems before a cryptographically-relevant quantum computer arrives. We provide a hybrid project management approach in *Quantum Cybersecurity Program Management* to enable migration to post-quantum cryptography (PQC), provide cryptographic agility, and implement other critical quantum computing projects (summarized in Figure 1.2).

Quantum Computers

Quantum algorithms are powered by quantum computers. There are multiple types of quantum computers. First, quantum annealers are available today and are the least powerful quantum computer. They face decoherence, noise, and calibration issues resulting in low adoption. The second category of quantum computing is analog quantum simulators that are specialized computers that simulate the behavior of quantum systems, molecules and materials in the fields of chemistry, physics, and materials science. However, they are at risk of noise and errors. Quantum computers form the third and most promising category of computers. These are challenging to build and require many qubits to become a useful and reliable quantum computer.

Benefits of Quantum Computing

Organizations are enticed by the capabilities and benefits of quantum computing, and many are revisioning their strategies to leverage these transformative technologies. Expect to see business cases appear in the annual budget cycle to adopt quantum technologies with the following rationale:

Increased speed: Some calculations can be performed faster due to quantum parallelism (where quantum qubits can exist in multiple states simultaneously). Shor's and Grover's algorithms leverage quantum parallelism to perform exponentially faster (e.g., factoring calculations). As quantum computers become more mature and stable with faster quantum processors, quantum computing will provide new business opportunities triggering requests for quantum technology projects.

Combinatorial optimization: an operations research field where one finds the optimal solution for a discrete set of options to maximize (e.g., select from a series of business opportunities to generate the most value) and/or minimize (e.g., the duration of a complex project schedule[12]). Expect more quantum technology use cases leveraging combinatorial optimization capabilities from business functions like human resources, engineering, finance, procurement, and others to minimize and maximize their operational key performance indicators (KPIs) as quantum computer technologies mature.

Machine learning and data analysis: using quantum computing and specialized algorithms like Grover's algorithm can hyper accelerate quantum machine learning (QML) and data analysis tasks like classification, clustering, and pattern recognition when searching data sets. Expect

---

[12]In *Quantum Cybersecurity* we predict that project management and PMOs (project management offices) will be transformed with quantum combinatorial optimization capabilities including project portfolio optimization, project selection, bid and proposal development, cost/time trade-off analysis, critical path analysis and project scheduling, resource allocation, leveling, and optimization, risk management (identification, analysis, treatment, monitor and control), Monte Carlo simulations (true random number generation), quality control (testing), and other areas dear to project teams! Researchers will find a wide array of impactful research projects in applied combinatorial optimization. However, these use cases will likely require more powerful quantum technologies than the first batch of technologies that provide a quantum advantage over classical computing.

quantum technology use cases from marketing, diagnostic imaging, library services, legal, and other business functions where improved searching is desired.

These capabilities of quantum technologies form the basis of business cases and the innovation these technologies may bring.

Technical Challenges

Quantum computing faces technical challenges, such as decoherence, quantum noise, error correction, and scaling, that need to be resolved to be applied to meaningful, industrial problems. Overcoming hardware-related challenges—the quantum bottleneck—marks progress toward achieving a cryptographically-relevant quantum computer, which could introduce serious security risks or enable groundbreaking innovations. IT and security architects monitor these developments closely to manage emerging quantum-related risks.

As progress is made to overcome these obstacles, the demand for quantum computing and post-quantum cryptographic migrations are surging. Regular advancements indicate that overcoming these challenges is increasingly feasible. Once achieved, quantum advantage will emerge, where quantum computers outperform classical systems, leading to Q-Day—when RSA-2048 encryption may be compromised by a cryptographically-relevant quantum computer.

Dual Potentialities of Quantum Computing

Quantum technologies including quantum computing have dual potentialities. Technology in general can be used for positive and constructive purposes or negative and harmful purposes. For example, one can use AI to generate a quantum computing awareness course ("constructive") or to launch a threatening email campaign ("harmful"). The technology is neutral; it is the user that determines whether to use the technology in a "good" way or in a "bad" way.

Therefore, organizations are preparing for the dual potentialities of quantum technologies by updating their organization's strategies. Organizational strategies with quantum goals will lead to quantum technology use case proposals with requests for approval and funding. The innovative capabilities are detailed in quantum technology use cases (e.g., quantum computing) and including the need to protect the organization against quantum threats with PQC.

To conclude, quantum technologies bring transformational promises and great risk. While these technologies are foundationally different from classical computing technologies, quantum technologies can be simplified as hardware (e.g., quantum computing), software (e.g., quantum algorithms), and integration with other subsystems (including classical computers) to create a hybrid digital ecosystem. To plan, implement, and optimize quantum technologies, it is best practice to begin with updating organizational strategies to leverage these new technologies.

Microlearning

Quantum computing is evolving from being the domain of scientists, engineers, and programmers in research centers to becoming desired technologies organizations are adopting. Find more information online about:

- Quantum milestones, past and future like Q-Day and Encryptogeddon,
- Current and future off-the-shelf algorithms that are emerging in your discipline,
- The difference between dual potentialities of technology and dual-use technologies,
- What are organizations doing to prepare for a cryptographically-relevant quantum computer?

CHAPTER 3

Begin with a Quantum Strategy

> *Sound strategy starts with having the right goal.*
>
> Michael Porter

It is best practice to begin the quantum technologies journey by updating the organization's most relevant strategies including their business, technology, and cybersecurity strategies. That is, formally prepare for the dual potentialities of quantum technologies: adopt transformative innovations and prevent quantum risks (e.g., treat with robust cryptographic agility). These strategies will detail whether the organization will use the "big bang" approach and implement a comprehensive program of quantum technology projects or perhaps begin with smaller learning experiments and proof of concept projects.

A common approach to updating strategies and making technological optimizations is to conduct a gap analysis (Figure 1.2) and identify the organization's current and target states. The gaps are elaborated and prioritized into a program of quantum technology projects. The organizational strategies (business, technology, and cybersecurity) can include any special requirements like implementing these technologies (especially PQC) as soon as possible.

Gap Analysis: Current State

Conducting a gap analysis is a common business practice and has been part of MBA curricula for decades. Similarly, the NIST Cybersecurity Framework guides the reader to conduct a cybersecurity gap analysis to improve their cybersecurity posture (NIST 2024a, 7). In this book, the

NIST gap analysis is loosely applied as it is a global cybersecurity framework and a significant amount of the program of quantum technology projects involve cybersecurity. Therefore, aligning with the NIST Cybersecurity Framework or others reduces risks and contributes to a shared understanding of the work ahead. The NIST gap analysis is combined with the ITIL approach to gap analysis since both are technology oriented.

The organization can analyze its current quantum objectives and capabilities (e.g., technical maturity detailed later and includes project, change, service, and cybersecurity management maturity). Organizations first determine their *current state* profile (Figure 3.1). The current state or profile includes the outcomes the organization is currently achieving or attempting to achieve and a measure of the degree of achievement.

Then the target state or profile is determined for where the organization wants to be with quantum technologies and innovation, as well as their quantum cybersecurity capabilities (e.g., quantum-safe cryptography and effective cryptographic agility). In Figure 3.1, two projects are required to progress from the current to the target state and close the gaps identified in the gap analysis. The gap analysis is greatly enhanced by applying Mosca's Theorem.

Mosca's Theorem

An early and critical question to ponder is how much time is available for the organization to implement quantum-safe solutions and achieve

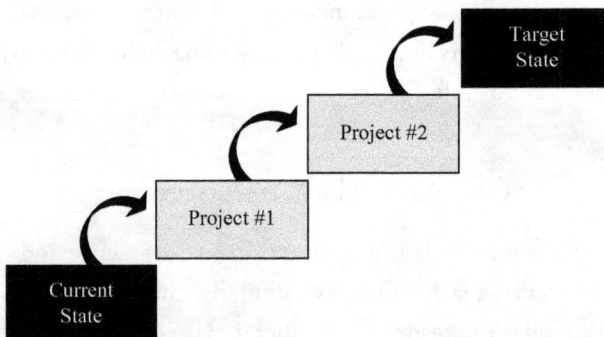

Figure 3.1 Quantum program current and target states

sufficient cryptographic agility. Michele Mosca and his research team developed a quantum timeline risk analysis approach represented mathematically (Mosca and Piani 2024).

Mosca's Theorem $(X + Y) > Z$

According to Mosca's Theorem $(X + Y) > Z$, when the amount of time that data must remain secure (X) plus the project time it takes to achieve sufficient post-quantum cryptographic protection (Y) is greater than when cryptographically-relevant quantum computers become available and powerful enough to break classical cryptography (Z), the organization has run out of time and their systems and data are at risk.[13] Organizations apply Mosca's Theorem to analyze risks and consider (Figure 3.2).

A goal of our previous book, *Quantum Cybersecurity Program Management,* is to assist readers to plan, implement, and optimize a program of quantum technology projects (adkAr) including post-quantum cryptographic migrations (Mosca's Y parameter). The goal of this book is to accelerate the front-end or pre-project phase where organizational change management begins (ADKar) and to improve the probability of implementing quantum-safe cryptography before a cryptographically-relevant computer emerges and finds its way into the hackers' arsenal.

Data security duration (X): organizations begin their quantum risk analysis by understanding how long encryption is needed to secure their data sets[14] (Figure 3.2). Organizations have multiple data sets like personally identifiable information and corporate intellectual property, with varying degrees of sensitivity and criticality. Some data must be kept secure for only a few years, like credit card information that is relevant until the card's expiration date, then the value of the data declines with time. Medical data and other data might be relevant for decades as directed by regulatory bodies, requiring more extended periods of protection for

---

[13]Readers may pause, re-read this paragraph, and reflect upon this critical and indispensable risk analysis technique that guides the quantum strategy and program of projects.

[14]See *Quantum Cybersecurity* for a comprehensive description of data sets that may be at risk.

Scenario #1: Early Start   **Scenario #2: Late Start**

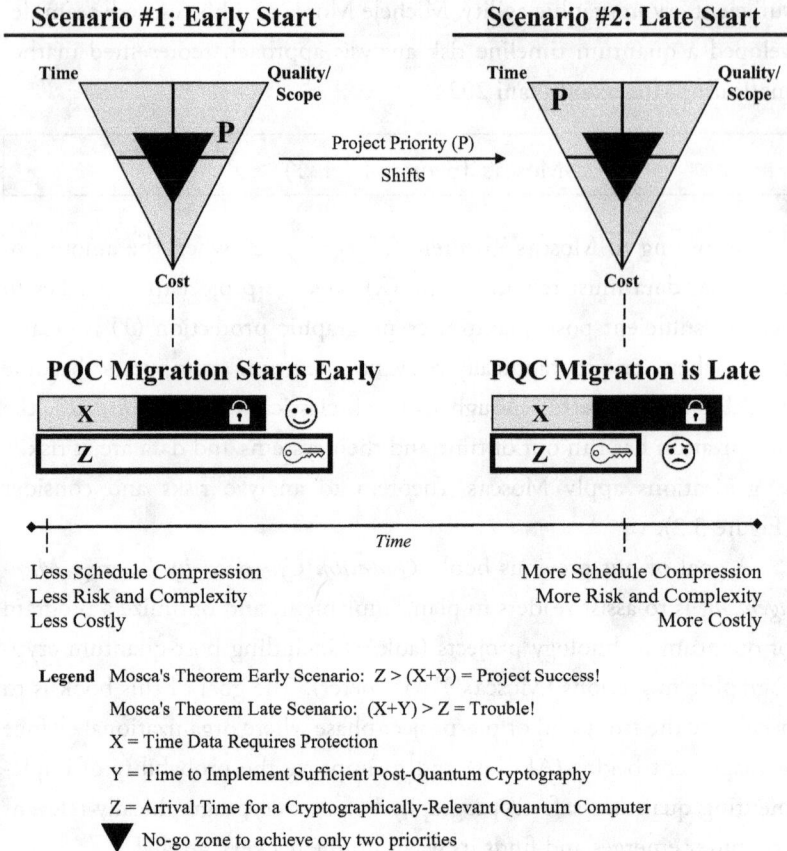

Figure 3.2 Post-quantum cryptographic migration project priority

up to 50 years (Canadian Forum for Digital Infrastructure Resilience 2023, 5). Organizations can prioritize their data sets (e.g., data classified as "high value assets" or their "crown jewels") for protection beginning in the strategy phase and elaborated in the project plan and design phases of quantum technology projects.

Project time to implement PQC (Y): the project team is tasked to answer the most dreaded question in project management: "How long will it take?" And in a quantum cybersecurity risk analysis, the organization estimates the time to migrate to quantum-safe cryptography (e.g., NIST approved post-quantum cryptographic algorithms) to protect and secure prioritized data and systems. The post-quantum cryptographic algorithms are like robust locks that secure the organization's data and systems against a cryptographically-relevant quantum computer. The migration time is dependent upon the technical maturity of the organization and the competence of the quantum project teams. Estimating activity durations for complex activities is the purview of project schedule management and we have detailed that process and tools in *Cybersecurity Project Management* (Skulmoski 2022). Our previous book—*Quantum Cybersecurity Program Management*—provides an approach to manage the Y parameter in Mosca's Theorem.

Time to a cryptographically-relevant quantum computer (Z): the third parameter in Mosca's Theorem (Figure 3.2) represents the time until a cryptographically-relevant quantum computer arrives that can break public-key encryption typically used by classical computers. The cryptographically-relevant quantum computer is like the keys that can unlock the organization's most sensitive data and disrupt systems operations. There is a degree of uncertainty to when a cryptographically-relevant quantum computer may arrive and is one of the key milestones tracked by quantum champions.

The Z parameter is external to organizations and out of their control. IT and security architects monitor technological milestones like quantum computer processor progress. They also monitor perhaps the most impactful milestone: when a cryptographically-relevant quantum computer may break the 2048-bit RSA key[15] (Q-Day). Mosca and Piani (2024) research the quantum threat timelines and produce progress reports to help quantum champions predict the arrival of a cryptographically-relevant quantum computer. It is like a cyber arms race to install quantum-resistant *locks* before quantum *keys* are available to hackers.

Therefore, the organization analyzes the degree their data sets and systems are vulnerable to a cyber-attack with a cryptographically-relevant quantum computer and the urgency to protect data (personal and organizational) and systems; in essence, "how long does the data need to

---

[15]It would take around 300 trillion years for a classical computer to break an RSA-2048 bit encryption key when one searches online for estimates. We are less interested in a precise number (200 to 300 trillion or even one billion years is still a lot of time required to hack into a computer), and instead we are more interested in the order of magnitude required to break classical public encryption with a cryptographically-relevant quantum computer.

be protected?" Mosca guides organizations to conduct an internal risk assessment (data security duration and project transition timelines to PQC) and an external risk assessment (arrival time of a cryptographically-relevant quantum computer). The technical leadership team analyzes the data, estimates the duration to migrate to PQC and predicts when a cryptographically-relevant quantum computer may arrive (Figure 3.2). Some might factor in additional time for post-quantum cryptographic migrations if their organization is not likely an immediate target (e.g., risk acceptance strategy) and not in a critical infrastructure industry like defense or healthcare.

For these reasons, key cybersecurity goals are to optimize and perhaps reduce the transition time to achieve sufficient PQC (Y). That is, organizations will benefit from a lean project-oriented approach to minimize the time to achieve cybersecurity readiness (PQC and cryptographic agility) should a cryptographically-relevant quantum computer arrive earlier than predicted.

As seen in Figure 3.2 (scenario #2), organizations will not be able to protect their systems and data from quantum attacks ($X + Y > Z$) if the quantum threat timeline for cryptographically-relevant quantum computers (Z) is shorter than the data security requirements (X) and transition project durations (Y). The risk register may be updated with a risk statement (Table 3.1) with potentially high impacts.

Thus, a severe risk (high probability and high impact) is a cryptographically-relevant quantum computer may emerge before an organization completes its post-quantum cryptographic migrations (the "Mosca Inequality"). Should an organization discover they do not have enough time for a complete transition to post-quantum cryptographic solutions and the time to a cryptographically-relevant quantum computer is imminent, then the quantum cybersecurity leadership team can prioritize systems and data (e.g., crown jewels) to protect so if the organization is successfully attacked with a quantum computer, perhaps only less sensitive and critical data might be exfiltrated or compromised. The organization can add extra resources and crash and fast track prioritized projects; however, schedule compression techniques are complex and risky.

Applying Mosca's Theorem ($X + Y) > Z$ indicates a late post-quantum cryptographic migration program (scenario 2, Figure 3.2), leaving the

Table 3.1 Q-Day risk statement

Risk statement	Description
Cause	Due to the growing investments, research and collaboration in quantum computing,
Risk	There is a risk a cryptographically-relevant quantum computer (Q-Day) may arrive sooner than anticipated,
Effect	Resulting in at least four potentially high-impact effects:[16] (i) the organization's data and systems are exposed to quantum risks sooner than expected; (ii) the available project time is reduced to implement minimum viable cybersecurity, post-quantum cryptographic migrations and cryptographic agility projects; (iii) a shortage of qualified quantum talent; and (iv) the available consultants may charge high fees (due to the high demand for quantum competencies).

organization exposed to risks (e.g., the classical public cryptographic keys can be broken). Some authorities suggest the migration timeline can easily take a decade (Canadian Forum for Digital Infrastructure Resilience 2023, 11–12). Thus, quantum champions monitor *Q-Day*: the arrival of a cryptographically-relevant quantum computer and include Mosca's risk assessment as part of their gap analysis.

Quantum champions, with organizational and executive support and sufficient technical maturity, can prevent and mitigate many quantum risks with a systematic approach based on best practices to complete post-quantum cryptographic migrations before a cryptographically-relevant quantum computer emerges (scenario 1, Figure 3.2). A decade of projects may be required to plan, implement, and optimize quantum-resistant cybersecurity; so, optimize change, project, and technology service management processes and tools (e.g., high technical maturity) found in standards and frameworks (addressed later in Table 4.1) as they represent generally accepted best practices that reduce risks and improve the probability of delivering the desired level of quality.

Therefore, there is a strong and convincing case to prepare for the quantum era of opportunities and threats. Indeed, hesitancy introduces

---

[16]It is good practice to include only one effect (and risk and cause) in the risk statement for better tracking. However, for simplicity purposes, the four effects are included in one risk statement.

the risk that when the organization desires post-quantum cryptographic migration consulting assistance, there may be a shortage of talent should early adopters have the best SMEs already engaged. The current generation of cybersecurity teams can learn from previous cryptographic migrations (e.g., replacing SHA-1[17] with SHA-2 hash functions) that also required long project timelines, like the long and complex post-quantum cryptographic migration timeline (Mosca 2024). A key lesson learned from previous migrations: Start early!

There is another severe risk that due to the desire to gain a strategic advantage, some research and development may be secret or covert, resulting in a cryptographically-relevant quantum computer emerging sooner than anticipated (scenario 2, Figure 3.2). Recall that ChatGPT arrived somewhat unexpectedly, and organizations responded with prioritized AI technology implementations. Again, initiating a quantum program of projects without delay can mitigate the risk of a cryptographically-relevant quantum computer arriving sooner than expected.

While the Mosca Theorem is a popular approach to analyzing the organization's quantum risks, the Crypto Agility Risk Management Framework (Ma et al. 2021) offers another approach should the organization desire financial decision-making data to guide their analysis. Once the team analyzes and agrees on Mosca's three parameters, they add any necessary schedule compression requirements to the quantum strategies for further consideration (Chapter 8).

Project Priority

An often neglected and critical step in crafting strategies and project plans is to clearly identify the priority and provide the rationale for the

---

[17]The SHA-1 algorithm for digital signatures was introduced in 1995 had design flaws that were only discovered in 2005 after it was widely adopted and used. In 2011, NIST recommended migrating to SHA-2. The initial post-quantum cryptographic algorithms approved by NIST might also have similar vulnerabilities discovered only after widespread adoption necessitating quick upgrades (e.g., cryptographic agility) to more secure post-quantum cryptography necessary for cryptographic agility. See Perryman et al. (2024) for more about previous cryptographic migrations (e.g., add to your cryptographic migration project lessons learned).

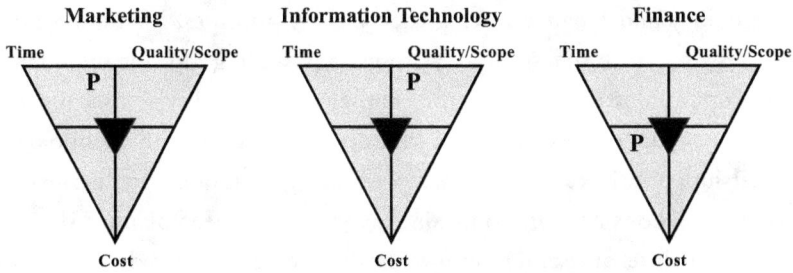

Figure 3.3 Project priority misalignment

organization's projects; it is also called the "case for change" in the *Standard for Change Management*. In change management, a strong case for change is critical for success. Once there is a shared understanding of the rationale for quantum technologies, determine the project priority.

The Priority Triangle tool helps the team to identify the project priorities. The Priority Triangle (Figure 3.3, Skulmoski and Hartman 2000) is adapted from Martin Barnes' classical Iron Triangle, also known as the Triple Constraint Theory (Kerzner 2013, 869). Project teams are constrained by scope, time, cost, and quality; a change in one constraint will affect the others. For instance, if a client asks to increase the scope of a quantum technologies project, the project team may face additional costs and schedule overruns due to "scope creep."

Project managers use the triple constraint theory to identify project priorities by emphasizing the key constraints of time, cost, and quality/scope. In a Priority Triangle,[18] time is positioned on the left as minimizing the project duration is often a goal; cost is at the bottom to signify budget control and quality/scope is on the right to optimize project value. However, since stakeholders often desire all these constraints, a "No-Go" zone is added in the center of the Priority Triangle, guiding key stakeholders to identify their top two project priorities ("P" in Figure 3.3).

Consider a use case where an organization wants to implement a QKD communications network to provide communication services between two nearby cities. There are stakeholders from Marketing, Information

---

[18]For more about using the Priority Triangle in planning and delivery, see *Quantum Cybersecurity Program Management*.

Technology and Finance voicing their project priorities. Marketing prioritizes *time* since they seek an as soon as possible go-live of the quantum communications network to begin sales, with quality as a secondary priority to support marketability. However, the Information Technology leadership prioritizes service *quality*, favoring a durable, maintainable communications network to maximize the time between planned downtime for maintenance and minimize the duration of planned downtime to complete maintenance activities. Finance prioritizes *cost* (staying within the project budget) with a timely completion as their second priority to start revenue generation. These varied priorities highlight misalignment among project stakeholders. The *approved* project priority is usually determined by the project funder and is often the project sponsor[19] with the approved budget to initiate the project.

In the QKD communications network example (Figure 3.3), the project sponsor officially prioritizes time then quality/scope, allowing the project manager flexibility with the budget. The approved project priority is documented in the project plan that authorizes the project manager to use strategies such as overtime to meet project priorities, even if it increases costs. The project manager closely monitors project progress and controls risks. If exceeding the budget becomes a risk, the project manager informs the sponsor and works to prevent and mitigate the risk before it becomes an issue. Project managers understand the importance of to "never surprise your boss" who can be both the project sponsor and PMO director for example. Throughout the QKD project, the project manager regularly validates whether project priorities remain the same or have shifted. The project priority can change in projects (Figure 3.2 from scenario 1 to 2) to finishing ASAP due to heightened risks (e.g., Q-Day) or the desire to finish the project.

Identifying, discussing and documenting the project priorities in the approved project plan aligns communications, manages expectations, and significantly reduces risks. Should the project priority be on time to such a degree that it becomes a compressed schedule project, then complete

---

[19]The project sponsor is also known as the product manager or service owner depending on the academic body of knowledge that has different terms for the same role!

additional analysis and planning to baseline and implement a feasible schedule. The quantum strategies will include the project priorities for the organization and any requirement for schedule compression.

Gap Analysis: Target State

The target state is simply the desired future; the state of the organization after the quantum program of projects have been planned and implemented to close the gap followed by continual[20] improvement initiatives after the technologies have been used. The target state will include objectives like migrating to NIST-approved PQC (NIST Dilithium) by a certain target date (e.g., December 2029). Collaborate with your finance team to determine financial objectives like return on investment, cost–benefit analysis, and other metrics to aid decision making to secure sustainable program funding. Identifying the target state is driven by developing quantum strategies during the pre-project phase (ADKar).

Quantum Strategies

The organization's quantum strategies address the dual potentialities of quantum technologies: leverage the positive aspects and implement strategies to treat quantum technology-related risks. Quantum strategic planning begins with the *business strategy* (Figure 3.4) that organizations update to include quantum technologies and their role in generating innovation and value for the organization. As departmental strategies evolve to include quantum technologies, update the *technology strategy* to support business goals. The *cybersecurity strategy* is also revised to align with quantum technology goals like post-quantum cryptographic migrations and cryptographic agility. These three strategies trigger projects that bring

---

[20]The terms continuous and continual improvement are similar, but what is the difference? Continuous improvement involves ongoing enhancements that do not stop. Continual improvement goes further, where organizations look externally to benchmark, innovate, and improve. Hence, in *Accelerated Quantum Technologies Change Management*, we use "continual improvement," as featured in the ISO 9001 Quality Management standard. Organizations are advised to monitor emerging standards and frameworks related to quantum technologies.

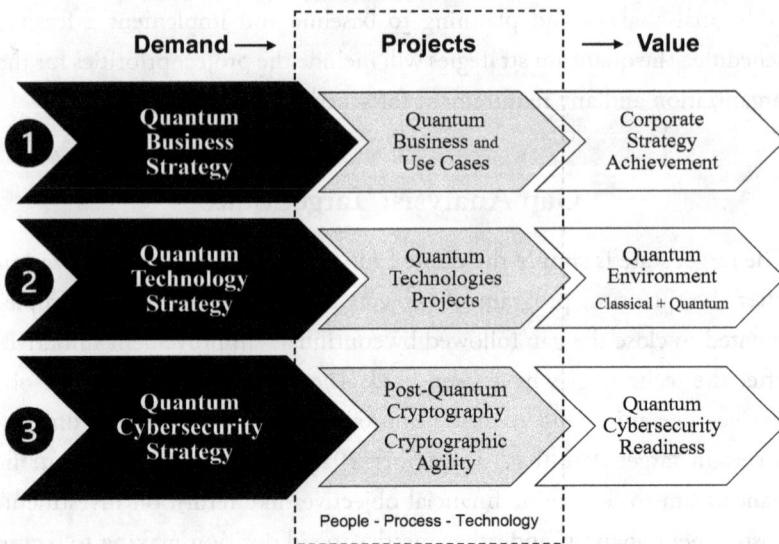

Figure 3.4 Quantum strategies alignment

the organization closer to their target state and deliver value using quantum technologies as described in the approved quantum technology use cases.

Guiding these strategic, project, and operational activities is a foundation of best practices represented in standards and frameworks. For example, align quantum computing projects with the PMBOK Guide for project management, the ITIL framework for technology service management, and the NIST Cybersecurity Framework to define the organization's target cybersecurity profile in support of post-quantum cryptographic migration. Analysts then conduct a feasibility analysis— including an assessment of technical maturity—as a fundamental task when evaluating the target state.

Can We Do It? A Quantum Technical Maturity Assessment

An early question to ask and discuss when examining the feasibility of adopting quantum technologies during strategic planning is "can we do it?" That is, does the organization have sufficient technical maturity capabilities—project, change, service, and cybersecurity management maturity—to implement their updated business, technology, and cybersecurity strategies? Begin with an audit of the different types of technical maturity and apply and tailor a formal auditing process like ISO 19011:2018 Guidelines for Auditing Management Systems to determine feasibility.

Project management maturity: the capability level in project management processes, systems, and tools. There are many project management maturity models like the Organizational Project Management Maturity Model from the Project Management Institute to guide progressive improvements in project management processes and tools (e.g., develop a lean project approval process for post-quantum cryptographic migrations).

Cybersecurity maturity: the organization's level of cybersecurity capabilities. An example of a cybersecurity maturity model is the Cybersecurity Capability Maturity Model (C2M2) that was developed by American energy management SMEs to guide cybersecurity capability improvements. The reasoning to strive for sufficient cybersecurity maturity is the large scope of work involved in post-quantum cryptographic migrations and cryptographic agility projects.

Service management maturity: the organization's level of technology service management capabilities throughout the technology life cycle. Given that quantum technologies will bring significant digital change and promise, organizations can streamline their end-to-end technology management processes beginning with the demand for technology services like quantum, through to delivering quantum value to end users, then sunsetting legacy technologies displaced by quantum technologies. The popular ITIL and COBIT service management frameworks include maturity models to guide optimization projects and initiatives. Organizations can use these maturity models and others to evaluate their service management capabilities as part of their gap analysis.

Organizational change management maturity: the capability of an organization to quickly and successfully innovate in response to market forces. Organizational change management is facilitated when integrated with program and portfolio management (Skulmoski and Memari 2025a) and enterprise risk management (NIST 2020).

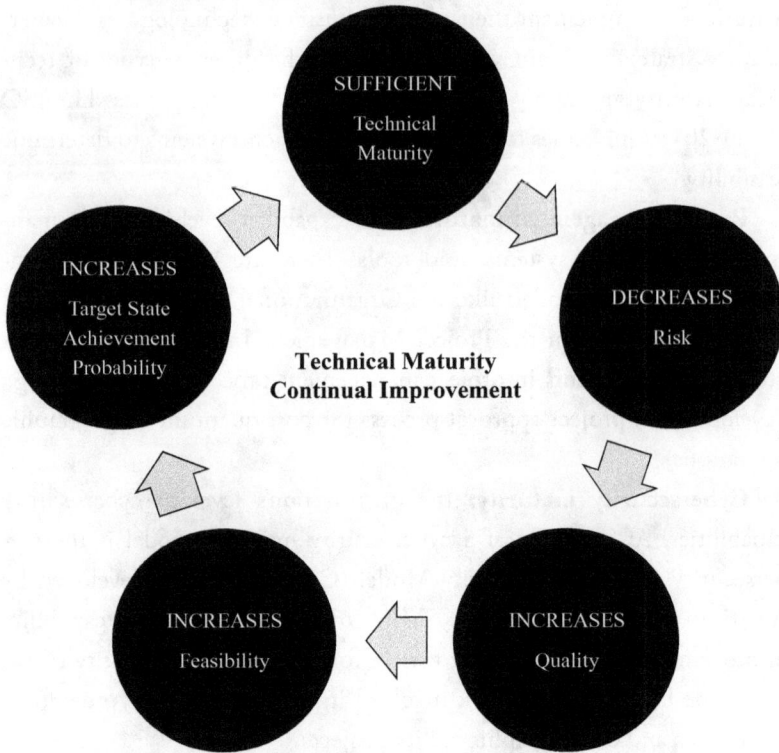

Figure 3.5 Technical maturity pathway

Continual and progressive improvement underlie these maturity models in that there is planned progress through projects to mature to a target state (Figure 3.1). Generally, organizations mature their technical capabilities to just enough to successfully accomplish their work (Figure 3.5). The right amount of technical maturity is likely a unique "sweet spot" for organizations described as the *Goldilocks Principle of Project Management* (Skulmoski 2022): not too much, not too little, but just the right amount.[21] With sufficient technical maturity, digital projects

---

[21]In a Nineteenth-Century fairy tale Goldilocks, the main character, did not want too much, nor too little; Goldilocks always wanted just the right amount. Therefore, the *Goldilocks Principle* strives to apply not too much, nor too little technical maturity, just the right amount to be successful. However, the moral of the *Goldilocks and the Three Bears* fairy tale is not to enter someone's home (or digital ecosystem) without their permission.

Table 3.2 Technical maturity capability Gizmo

Technical maturity stack	Rate, discuss, and act	Rating High	Low
Project management maturity	What is the level of project management maturity for this organization or department?	5 – 4 – 3 – 2 – 1	
Cybersecurity management maturity	What is the level of cybersecurity maturity for this organization or department?	5 – 4 – 3 – 2 – 1	
Technology service management maturity	What is the level of service management maturity for this organization or department?	5 – 4 – 3 – 2 – 1	
Organizational change management maturity	What is the level of organizational change management maturity for this organization or department?	5 – 4 – 3 – 2 – 1	

involving quantum technologies are less likely to encounter risks, and are more likely to achieve the desired quality, feasibility, and target state. While the journey to the target state may imply linearity, indeed, the work is iterative and continuous leading organizations to progressively pursue target states through a program of projects and smaller initiatives.

The key benefit of all these models is they guide organizations to swiftly respond and adapt to change. Thus, analyze the technical capability of an organization to plan, implement,[22] and optimize quantum technologies from multiple perspectives with the Technical Maturity Gizmo (Table 3.2).

The main purpose of this and any Gizmo is to initiate engagement and guide discussions so that there is a shared understanding of the concepts under consideration. Ideally, the discussions will generate follow-up actions, and in this case, perhaps process optimization projects to smooth the way for quantum technologies adoption (see the Appendixes for more about Gizmos and workshops).

---

[22]In this book, the "plan and implement" project phases are shortened for convenience and include the initiate, plan, design, build/configure, test, transition to production, go-live, and close out phases. Optimization usually occurs after the project deliverables are used and opportunities to improve are identified, prioritized, and scheduled for optimization.

Technical maturity can be seen as a *stack* of best practices to support a program of quantum technology projects (Table 3.2). The organization can combine other maturity models from their own industries (e.g., port management, green energy engineering or pharmacy operations) to their technical maturity stack to streamline processes ahead of the program of quantum technology projects to follow.

For each technical maturity element in the stack, conduct a gap analysis to guide future optimization projects (Figure 1.2). Many gaps can be addressed with technical maturity optimization projects in the program of projects; that is, improve the probability of success by maturing the organizations processes and tools to achieve the target state for quantum technologies.

Desired Degree of Schedule Compression

An early strategic decision is to determine the degree of schedule compression required (target) based on Mosca's risk assessment and the project priority. Mosca's Theorem is applied to see if schedule compression is required due to the arrival timing of a cryptographically-relevant quantum computer (e.g., it has arrived or is imminent—within the next five years). Using the Priority Triangle helps understand and identify the degree a project schedule may need to be compressed; if there is a high priority on finishing the project quickly, then schedule compression may be an appropriate technique *if* there is sufficient technical maturity and competency. These assessments can inform leadership of the degree of schedule compression required to meet quantum strategy targets: high, medium, or low/negligible compression.

Most projects face risks related to completing projects on time and some degree of schedule compression is often applied, especially at the tail-end of the project to finish early, on time or to minimize the amount of time the project goes beyond the approved schedule. Therefore, leadership guides project teams by indicating in their strategies (business, technology, and cybersecurity) the project priority and the amount of schedule compression the organization desires. This strategic information helps to clarify and elaborate the target state for the organization's quantum computing.

Business Strategy

Business strategies are regularly reviewed and revised, and at some point, quantum technologies become a strategic priority for an organization. A subset of the business strategy will include a quantum strategy. When developing a quantum strategy, determine the project type attributes: criticality, complexity, priority, and urgency.

> **Criticality:** relates to the importance of the quantum technology project to achieve the organization's goals and objectives.
>
> **Complexity:** the degree of difficulty to plan, manage, and implement a quantum technology project. Add any constraints, assumptions, and risks that can increase complexity.
>
> **Priority:** the project's level of importance to the organization and in relationship with other projects.
>
> **Urgency:** how sensitive the timing is to implement quantum technologies; meaning how quickly does the project need to be completed?

Evaluate and document the criticality, complexity, priority, and urgency for your organization to adopt quantum technologies (Table 3.3). The point is not to arrive at a precise score but rather as a discussion vehicle to develop awareness and alignment for the program of quantum technology projects followed up with actions to advance the strategy (e.g., ADKar type of actions).

While the Quantum Technologies Adoption Readiness Gizmo (Table 3.3) is used at the organizational level, it can be tailored for the department or unit level. For example, an engineering team may start their quantum journey by asking, "What level of priority are quantum technology projects to our engineering department?" followed by an action-oriented discussion of where there is rating agreement and variability.

It is good practice to plan, implement, and review strategy including schedule compression objectives throughout the delivery of the quantum program of projects since the strategic determinants may change over the course of project delivery (Figure 3.6). Here, the quantum and compression strategies also align with ADKar in that creating awareness, desire,

Table 3.3 Quantum technologies project evaluation Gizmo

Project type attributes	Rate, discuss, and act	Rating High Low
Criticality	a) What level of criticality to the organization is it to innovate (e.g., optimize or simulate) with quantum technologies?	5 – 4 – 3 – 2 – 1
	b) To what degree are the organization's systems and data susceptible to an attack with a cryptographically-relevant quantum computer?	5 – 4 – 3 – 2 – 1
Complexity	a) How difficult will it be for the organization to innovate with quantum technologies?	5 – 4 – 3 – 2 – 1
	b) How demanding will it be to complete the projects to protect the organization's systems and data from a quantum cybersecurity attack?	5 – 4 – 3 – 2 – 1
Priority	What is the level of importance of the project to the organization and in relationship with other projects?	5 – 4 – 3 – 2 – 1
Urgency	How sensitive is the timing to implement quantum technologies as outlined in the organization's approved strategies (e.g., business, information technology, and cybersecurity strategies)?	5 – 4 – 3 – 2 – 1

Strategy Development, Planning and Execution are Iterative

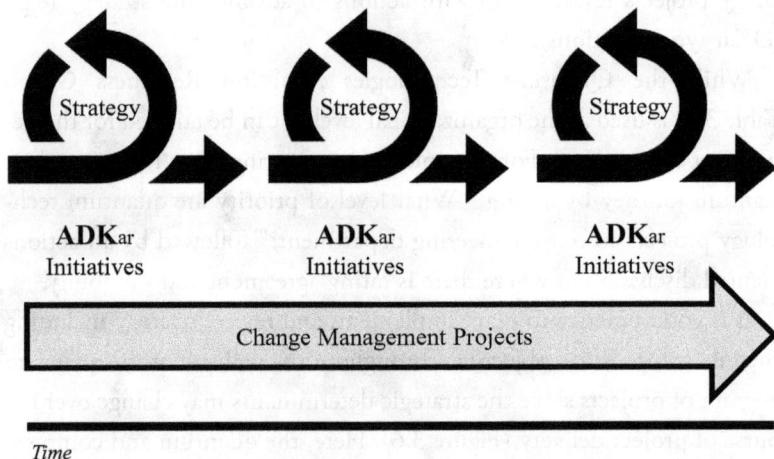

Figure 3.6 Ongoing strategy planning, implementing, and feedback iterations

and knowledge is also ongoing; that is, strategies are progressively elaborated (more detail is added over time).

There are many ways to develop strategies for quantum technologies like those taught in business schools. In this book, the ITIL Service Management framework (Axelos 2020) is applied and tailored to quantum technology change and project management. The ITIL framework guides technology life cycle management and is process-based designed to minimize risks and deliver the required level of quality. It includes 34 technology management practices like Strategy Management, Project Management, Risk Management, and Capacity and Performance Management. Combine the ITIL Service Management framework with other leading standards and frameworks like change management (ADKar) and project management (e.g., PRINCE2) to quantum technology projects. Add cybersecurity best practices (e.g., NIST Cybersecurity Framework) if the project scope includes cybersecurity.

Functional units like manufacturing, pharmacy, human resources, supply chain, government services, oncology research, and others respond to business strategies with use cases that propose new and/or optimized products and services with quantum technologies.

Quantum Technology Use Cases

Quantum technology uses cases may be on a continuum of technical (e.g., protein folding simulation research) through to nontechnical quantum technology use cases (e.g., quantum awareness mentoring for the organization's leadership). A nontechnical quantum technology use case may include the purpose, audience, need or business problem, expected benefits, scope of work, key risks and issues, and success criteria. A technology use case is a way to identify, elaborate and document system requirements to complete a task like automating a process to protect systems from a cybersecurity attack. Developing and following a use case template improves quality, understanding, and communications, and reduces completion time. Quantum computing use cases can also be developed for broad societal and global impacts like progress toward solving wicked problems and attaining Sustainable Development Goals (SDGs).

Sustainable Development Goals: The United Nations proclaimed 2025 as the *International Year of Quantum Science and Technology* due to the transformative capabilities that may be possible with these technologies. The World Economic Forum urges organizations to "prepare now" as quantum technologies can accelerate progress toward the SDGs made possible through quantum technologies (WEF 2024, 8).

Healthcare: Quantum computing in healthcare holds great promise and one of the early adopters is the Cleveland Clinic, the United States, where drug discovery is accelerated through simulations and ongoing research to earlier detection of lung cancer using quantum algorithms with a simple blood test and other biomarkers. Quantum computing can be used to improve hospital operation flows with combinatorial optimization algorithms tuned for quantum computing. Common workflows—such as those in pharmacies and pathology labs—aim to minimize throughput times and waste while maximizing the interval between unplanned medical equipment downtime made possible through optimized maintenance. The hospital's finance department may also use quantum computing to minimize the patient's out-of-pocket expenses and maximize the amount insurers pay for the medical services (Skulmoski and Memari 2025b).

Defense and space: the defense and space infrastructures have many promising quantum technology applications like improved state, military, and defense communications. Adversaries routinely target communications to eavesdrop[23] and gain strategic and tactical advantage. Quantum computing will allow vast amounts of data to be accurately and quickly analyzed as inputs to military and defense strategies and tactics. Quantum sensing technologies would enable earlier detection of threats like missiles and aircraft. QKD will also be used in the space sector for secure communications.

---

[23]An example of a major eavesdropping attack is the Volt Typhoon cyber espionage campaign attributed to a hacking group linked to China. Detected in May 2023, the attack targeted critical infrastructure organizations in the United States, including telecommunications, energy, transportation, and water sectors. The attackers used stealthy techniques, such as *living-off-the-land* tactics, which involve leveraging legitimate tools and system administration commands to avoid detection. They focused on long-term access rather than immediate disruption, aiming to gather intelligence and maintain persistence.

Public sector: These use cases improve government services like optimizing supply chains, social services, public transportation, and education. For instance, the New South Wales government in Australia has launched a long-term quantum computing program to optimize their state's public transportation system to reduce costs and unplanned downtime, and to optimize passenger throughput (NSW Government 2024).

These use cases once approved and funded can be implemented following best practices outlined in standards and frameworks and constrained or enabled by the technical maturity of the organization. Some uses cases can benefit from the first wave of quantum technologies, while others will benefit from later generations of these technologies.

Like most technology life cycles, quantum technologies progress through phases. An early phase is the Noisy Intermediate Quantum Era, followed by the Quantum Era, then the Optimized Quantum Era. As of the writing of this book (2025), the world was in the Noisy Intermediate Quantum Era (prior to Q-Day). The Quantum Era will arrive with the introduction of a quantum computer that can solve practical problems faster than classical computers (e.g., the quantum advantage). With sufficient technological maturity, extremely complex, perplexing, and wicked problems will be addressed with advanced techniques like combinatorial optimization that will signal the Optimized Quantum Era.

Microlearning

Look online for more information about strategy development:

- Find quantum technology optimization use cases for your department or discipline based on the QUBO algorithm for job shop scheduling problems,
- Search for how others are using quantum computing, quantum sensing, and quantum communications to gain a better appreciation for the diversity of quantum technology use cases and how they might apply to your organization,
- What wicked problems exist in your discipline and industry?
- Find out how progressive elaboration works and how it is applied to strategy and change management planning and execution.

Technology Strategy

A technology strategy updated for quantum technologies uses the organization's business strategy as its guiding input. The purpose of the technology strategy is to enable business objectives outlined in the organization's approved quantum technology uses cases and the transition to a hybrid ecosystem with classical and quantum computing technologies. Organizations benefit from developing a quantum technology strategy guided by standards and frameworks like ITIL or COBIT technology service management since providing quantum technologies is a service like other technologies. Use change management practices like ADKar to collaborate with other stakeholders to develop strategies and quantum technology use cases.

Cybersecurity Strategy

The cybersecurity strategy uses the organization's business and technology strategies as its principal input. The purpose of the cybersecurity strategy is to guide the organization to manage its cybersecurity risks. It may emphasize establishing a minimum viable cybersecurity foundation, followed by a cryptography inventory and initiating post-quantum cryptographic migrations and cryptographic agility projects and initiatives leading to cybersecurity readiness.

Organizations can benefit from developing a quantum cybersecurity strategy again by following best practices (e.g., NIST Cybersecurity Framework, ETSI standards, and the BSI standards). Use change management approaches to collaborate with other stakeholders (internal and external) in cybersecurity use cases and projects.

Developing a cybersecurity strategy for quantum technologies may be a daunting undertaking; however, the NIST gap analysis process (NIST Cybersecurity Framework 2024a) informs strategy development by identifying the target state. Gap analysis best practices identify the organization's current and target states regarding its technical maturity or capabilities to implement quantum technologies (e.g., change, project, technology service, and cybersecurity management maturity).

The first step to update the cybersecurity strategy is to determine the organization's capabilities and capacity to implement PQC and develop and maintain cryptographic agility (after establishing a solid cybersecurity foundation to protect against the "steal now, decrypt later" risk). The next step is conducting an impact analysis: What is the impact to the organization's data, systems, and privacy if a post-quantum cryptographically-relevant computer is used by a threat actor to gain unauthorized access to the organization's systems and data? The impact analysis may return the recommendation that the organization is behind implementing PQC and should proceed as quickly as possible (see also Mosca's Theorem and the Priority Triangle). In this case, the organization may investigate the degree of schedule compression to apply to their prioritized post-quantum cryptographic migrations and other projects.

To sum up this chapter, introduce quantum technologies and migrate to PQC, by updating the organization's business, technology, and cybersecurity strategies to start the quantum journey (Figure 3.7). Begin by evaluating the demand for quantum technologies, followed by a gap analysis, risk assessments, and project prioritization. A key determination is the degree the project schedule needs to be compressed if any. However, the probability of project success, let alone in a compressed schedule project is dependent upon technical maturity. Follow and tailor these steps to develop the organization's quantum strategies.

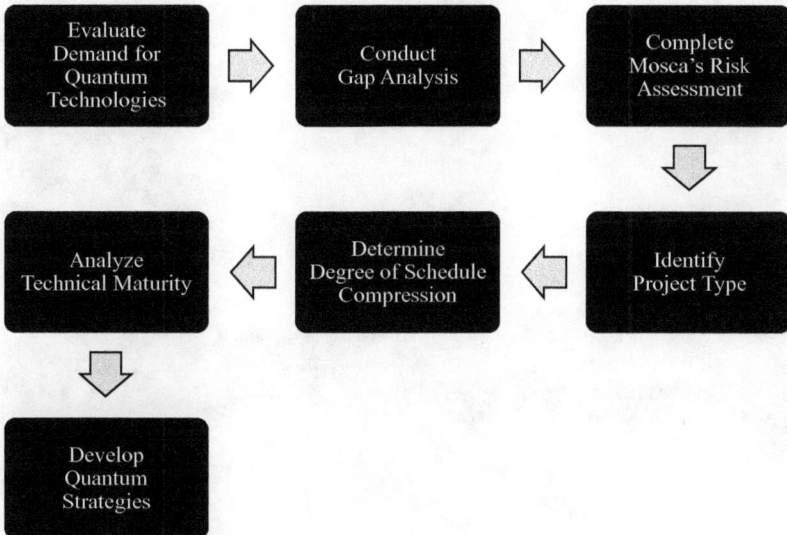

Figure 3.7 Quantum strategy development process

Microlearning

There are additional online supports and information about technical and cybersecurity strategies:

- Find technical and cybersecurity strategy templates and check-lists for quantum technologies,
- See how ITIL's Continual Improvement practice and the Change Enablement practice can be used in the quantum technologies gap analysis,
- Learn about technical and cybersecurity strategy best practices and lessons learned.

CHAPTER 4

Quantum Technology Program Management

> *I have always found that plans are useless, but planning is indispensable.*
>
> Dwight Eisenhower, 1962

Organizations are developing a suite of business, technology, and cybersecurity strategies that include quantum technologies. These strategies guide quantum business cases that are approved, funded, and implemented through a program of prioritized quantum technology projects (Figure 1.2). A critical success factor at this early stage of the organization's quantum journey is leadership support for quantum strategies aligned with organizational goals. Weak alignment and support diminishes the desire and engagement for quantum technologies and reduces the probability of a successful quantum program of projects. To address these risks, planning needs to be ongoing for the quantum program of projects.

There are many ways to organize quantum technology projects representing their dual potentialities: projects to deliver innovative products and services for the organization, and cybersecurity projects to protect the organization's data and systems from classical and quantum cyberattacks. Organizations may follow the standard gap analysis approach detailed in standards and frameworks that guide documenting their current and target states. To achieve the target state, organizations can initiate a program of projects and smaller initiatives. Technical maturity projects (project, technology, organizational change, and cybersecurity management) may first be initiated to optimize the process and tools used in the decade of quantum technology projects to follow. Organizations may customize their program of quantum technology projects—adding, removing, or

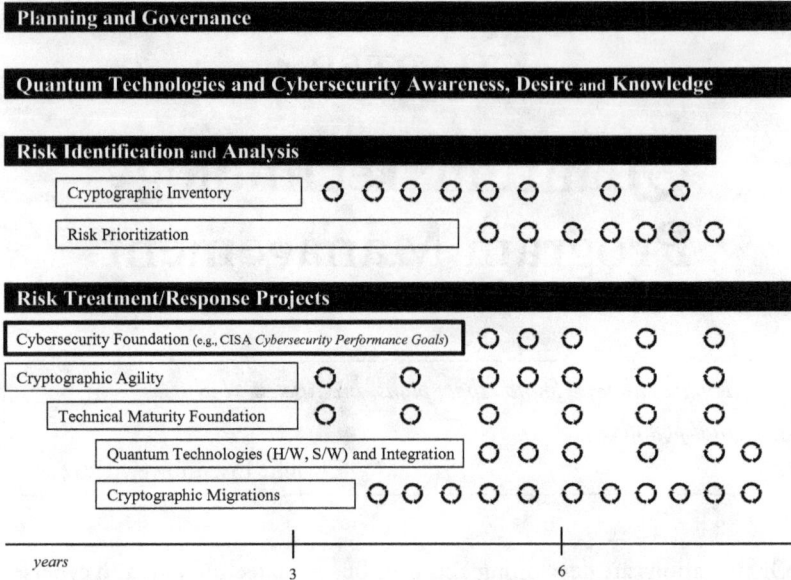

Figure 4.1 Program Gantt chart for quantum technology projects

adjusting—to align with their specific needs, as represented in a tailored quantum technologies program Gantt chart. (Figure 4.1, Skulmoski and Memari 2025a).

Quantum technology projects are complex. What is a complex[24] project? Searching online brings many definitions of project complexity that might be characterized by challenges to understand and predict how the project may unfold and difficulties to keep project activities under control. Complex projects like large-scale change management projects often involve many parts, people, and/or equipment that require tight coordination. Use the Technical Maturity Capability Gizmo (Table 3.2) to evaluate the organization's technical capabilities that contribute to complex project coordination. One of the benefits of program management is it is ideally suited to manage complexity. Begin with planning and establish

---

[24]As a student of history and thinking about the definition of a complex project, I am reminded of the *Meese Commission* to study the impact of pornography on American society in 1964 where the commission participants struggled to define and agree upon the definition of pornography. Justice Potter J. Stewart did not define pornography but stated, "I know it when I see it." Project complexity is similarly difficult to define but can be quickly recognized.

governance for the program of projects, then solidify the organization's cybersecurity foundation.

Cybersecurity Minimum Foundation

There are two reasons to develop a cybersecurity minimum foundation. First, the decade of cybersecurity projects to develop cryptographic agility (e.g., cryptographic inventories and post-quantum cryptographic migrations) benefit from a lean cybersecurity foundation rooted in best practices. Such a foundation enables organizations to scale their projects to prevent and mitigate emerging quantum threats while maintaining operational integrity. Organizations may assess their current cybersecurity maturity and identify any gaps that may hinder the journey to cryptographic agility. Addressing these gaps through targeted remediation strengthens the organization's cybersecurity resilience and enables a smoother transition to quantum-secure architectures. A minimum cybersecurity foundation is not only a prerequisite for quantum readiness—but it also streamlines ongoing projects and accelerates the adoption of secure technologies.

Second, many organizations are proactively addressing the "steal now, decrypt later" threat by establishing and continually improving a minimum viable cybersecurity foundation through focused projects and initiatives. Quantum cybersecurity efforts are increasingly centered on protecting data in use, at rest, and in transit from potential future decryption by quantum computers. For example, the daily transfer of backups across the public internet (data in transit) presents an immediate vulnerability. To mitigate this, organizations apply established cybersecurity frameworks such as the Essential Eight (Australian Signals Directorate 2022) and Cybersecurity and Infrastructure Security Agency's (CISA) Cybersecurity Performance Goals (2023). Short-term and tactical actions include implementing sprints to increase RSA key sizes to withstand brute-force attacks or adopting stronger hashing algorithms like SHA-512. While building and optimizing a robust cybersecurity foundation, organizations should also elevate awareness around the dual potentialities of quantum technologies—both as a threat and a transformative opportunity. While the minimum cybersecurity foundation is being established, initiate the broader change management project to build awareness of quantum technologies.

An early series of projects and initiatives is to develop awareness of the dual potentialities of quantum technologies: the *awareness* element of the Adkar change management phase. Given the complexity of the quantum program, the best-case scenario is for organizations to formally initiate change management awareness projects with engaged and sustained executive leadership support. Generating effective quantum technologies awareness can lead to desire, commitment, and enthusiasm to engage in the quantum journey. The quantum awareness project is further detailed in Chapter 6.

Technical Maturity Optimization

Ahead of implementing quantum technologies and migrating to PQC, the organization can optimize its processes and tools to improve the probability of successful projects for both quantum and classical technologies. Technical maturity comprises at least four related groups of processes and tools: (i) change management, (ii) project management, (iii) service management, and (iv) cybersecurity management maturity (Table 3.2). The value proposition of maturity models is as the organization progresses through the models, and judiciously applies and tailors their processes, risks are reduced, quality objectives are more likely achieved, and outcomes are predictable and repeatable. Therefore, organizations strive for a minimum viable foundation of technical maturity.

Organizations can improve technical maturity with lean processes (e.g., risk management), templates (e.g., quantum awareness program communications), checklists (e.g., PQC validation), and training (e.g., change management tool kits). Optimizing technical maturity ahead of quantum technology projects and initiatives can improve program delivery quality and reduce risks. See the Appendixes for the Detailed Technical Maturity Capability Gizmos.

Cryptographic Agility

The next category of projects is to achieve and maintain cryptographic agility: the ability to effectively respond to changing cryptographic threats with minimal disruption. Cryptographic agility is critical in the quantum era because the first version of NIST quantum algorithms were developed and released without testing their capabilities with a cryptographically-relevant quantum computer; indeed, it did not exist! Therefore, should vulnerabilities be identified in the early versions of PQC, then the organization will need to upgrade and perhaps replace cryptographic technologies to safeguard the organization's data and systems as they did with the migration from SHA-1 to SHA-2 algorithms.

The cryptographic response is holistic and enterprise-wide embodying its people, processes, and technologies, and is broader than the IT function. The organization's people are central to a secure organization and cryptographic agility requires its people to manage existing and future cybersecurity threats. The organization's processes are also updated for cryptographic agility. For instance, its policies, procedures, and contracts can support cryptographic agility where quantum susceptible technologies are no longer procured. Keeping cybersecurity technologies effective against threats requires cryptographic agility best practices like securing endpoint devices and effective port management. Thus, the organization may look at cryptographic agility as a strategic capability rather than an endpoint or goal.

Microlearning

Given there is constant change in organizations and technology, the project management, service management, cybersecurity management, and change management maturity frameworks can guide the organization's continual improvement actions.

- Look for project and service management resources (e.g., checklists and templates) tuned for your industry,
- Find out about project management maturity models like the OPM3 model from the Project Management Institute and service management maturity models from Axelos,
- Review the Cybersecurity Capability Maturity Model (C2M2) that is aligned with the NIST Cybersecurity Framework.

Quantum Technologies

The business units in organizations will request more quantum technologies outlined in use cases to deliver quantum-generated value (e.g., optimize the unit's KPIs or improve search capabilities). Quantum technologies can be managed with a technology management framework like ITIL where use cases are funded and approved that are aligned with the organization's quantum strategies. To implement the business' use cases, technologies are initiated, planned, and delivered to the project sponsor following the PMO's optimized project delivery approach previously tuned for quantum technology projects (e.g., technical maturity optimization projects, Figure 1.2). The quantum technology projects to support business use cases will often implement a minimum viable foundation of requirements (e.g., a "vanilla" installation) that delivers basic capabilities. Once the vanilla version of quantum technologies is delivered and used, requests for optimizations—such as scaling or additional functionality—are prioritized for future action.

Much like classical technologies (e.g., dot matrix printers), quantum technologies will follow a traditional life cycle of growth, maturity, and decline that can be managed with technology service management practices and processes. These business technology projects may occur

---

Microlearning

Cryptographic agility will become a strategic capability should the first generation of post-quantum cryptographic protocols need to be quickly and perhaps urgently updated to continue to protect the organization's systems and data.

- Generate a top five list of cryptographic agility best practices,
- Find out what your competitors and collaborators are doing to become cryptographically agile,
- Look for online templates that include contract clauses that outline post-quantum cryptographic requirements,
- Find examples of procurement policies and procedures tuned for cryptographic agility.

concurrently with cryptographic migrations, or they may be of a lesser priority where the organization prioritizes protecting its data and systems from quantum hackers.

Microlearning

Quantum technologies like quantum computing and sensors are broadly applicable with use cases across most industries (World Economic Forum 2024).

- What quantum sensors are being adopted in your city?
- What competencies are required to leverage quantum technologies in your industry?
- Where can you find SMEs with quantum technology competencies?

Post-Quantum Cryptographic Migrations

The post-quantum cryptographic migration projects are complex, delicate, and time-consuming (Mosca and Piani 2024). There are three main phases to cryptographic migrations (Figure 4.2) beginning with a cryptographic discovery inventory.

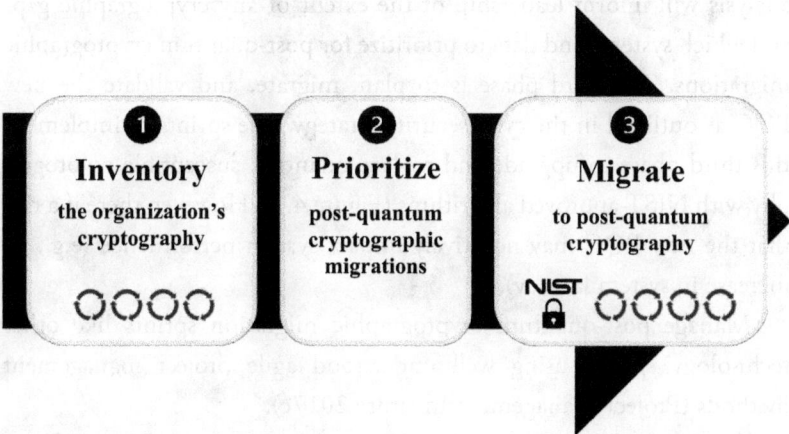

Figure 4.2 Three-phase post-quantum cryptographic migration

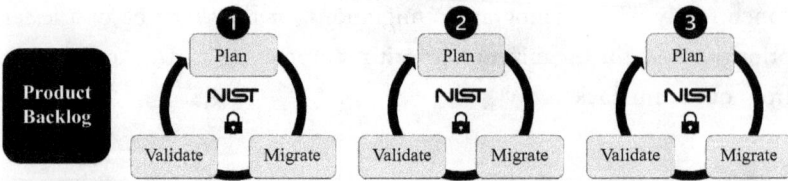

Figure 4.3 Post-quantum cryptographic migration sprints

First, the organization creates an inventory of its cryptography (cryptographic bill of materials) used in all systems, data, and processes through iterative audits. IT and cybersecurity teams will then evaluate quantum readiness across *internal* and *external* digital ecosystems including operational technologies (OT). The audit scope covers hardware (e.g., endpoint devices and firmware), software, and network connections including cloud technologies, with a focus on tracking cryptographic ownership and dependencies. Use Agile sprints to complete the discovery inventory. Use automated tools to find and document the organization's cryptography. But expect some manual auditing especially for legacy systems that does not support automated inventory tools.

After the organization creates a cryptographic inventory, the second phase is to analyze its current state of cryptography and to identify the cryptographic target state that a program of projects will deliver. The gap analysis will inform leadership of the extent of any cryptographic gaps and which systems and data to prioritize for post-quantum cryptographic migrations. The third phase is to plan, migrate, and validate the new PQC as outlined in the cybersecurity strategy. Use sprints to implement this third phase to upgrade and replace quantum susceptible cryptography with NIST-approved algorithms (Figure 4.3). However, there is a risk that the new PQC may negatively impact system performance (e.g., an increase in system latency).

Manage post-quantum cryptographic migration sprints like other technology sprints using well understood agile project management methods (Project Management Institute 2017c).

Microlearning

Organizations should develop expertise in post-quantum cryptographic migrations, as these projects may need to be repeated (e.g., cryptographic agility) if vulnerabilities are discovered in the initial NIST versions when faced with a cryptographically-relevant quantum computer. Consequently, developing and maintaining post-quantum cryptographic migration capabilities are essential.

- Are there regulatory requirements for post-quantum cryptographic migrations for your industry?
- What type of data in your industry is considered a high priority to protect with PQC?
- What cryptographic inventory tools and services are available?

Standards and Frameworks Alignment

Transitioning to quantum technologies and PQC benefits from a foundation of international standards and frameworks to reduce risks and improve the probability of delivering the required quality. While the standards and frameworks used in this book (Table 4.1) are globally accepted, they explicitly allow for tailoring and combining.

Organizations benefit from selecting additional standards and frameworks that align with their unique operational needs, guided by best practices in risk and quality management. However, no single framework fits all contexts and practitioners should use their discretion to tailor and combine standards and frameworks as necessary to establish a lean, sustainable foundation for the quantum technologies adoption work ahead. Recall that standards and frameworks are rarely implemented in their entirety; rather, organizations aim for a minimum viable foundation (e.g., their "sweet spot") of standards and frameworks that guide their business and project activities.

Thus, standards and frameworks contain best practices and are generally accepted and applicable to most organizations and projects, most of the time. Project managers bring the project management approach

Table 4.1 Quantum technology-related best practices

Best practices (partial list)	Technical maturity
A Guide to the Project Management Body of Knowledge (PMBOK Guide), Agile Practice Guide (PMI), The Standard for Program Management (PMI), PRINCE2 (project management from AXELOS), Praxis Framework (Australian Institute of Project Management), ISO 19011: 2018 Guidelines for Auditing Management Systems	Project Management
ITIL (Information Technology Infrastructure Library) for Service Management, COBIT (Control Objectives for Information and Related Technologies) Technology Governance Framework, ISO/IEC/IEEE 12207 Systems and Software Engineering—Software Life Cycle Processes	Service Management
Standard for Change Management (from the Association of Change Management Professionals), ISO/TS 10020:2022 Quality management systems—Organizational change management—Processes, Prosci ADKAR Change Management Model	Change Management
NIST Cybersecurity Framework, NIST Migration to Post-Quantum Cryptography: NIST SP 1800-38A Preliminary Draft, NIST IR 8286 Integrating Cybersecurity and Enterprise Risk Management (ERM), NIST SP 800-131A Rev. 2 Transitioning the Use of Cryptographic Algorithms and Key Lengths, ISO/IEC 27001 Information Security, Cybersecurity and Privacy Protection, Cybersecurity Capability Maturity Model (C2M2), ETSI standards, UK CSC standards	Cybersecurity Management
ISO 31000 Risk Management Series and ISO 9001 Quality Management	Supporting Standards

outlined in project management standards like the PMBOK Guide (Project Management Institute 2017a) and frameworks like the Scrum Guide (Schwaber and Sutherland 2020), and the SMEs they work with bring the design, standards, and frameworks from their disciplines (e.g., the quantum algorithm developer is guided by the ISO/IEC/IEEE 12207 Systems and Software Engineering—Software: Life Cycle Processes standard). Together, they create and hand over deliverables to the project sponsor (Figure 1.1). Since standards and frameworks bring generally accepted and precise vocabulary, their vocabulary is used in this book.

To conclude, there is a program of projects on the quantum technologies journey (Figure 1.2) including:

1. Quantum awareness projects to inform stakeholders of the dual potentialities of quantum technologies including a call to action;
2. Technical maturity optimization (project, service, change, and cybersecurity management maturity);
3. Cybersecurity foundation to protect against the "steal now, decrypt later" risk;
4. Cryptographic agility to be able to quickly upgrade the organization's cryptography with minimal disruption;
5. Quantum technologies and algorithms to support approved business cases;
6. Post-quantum cryptographic migrations to protect data and systems from a quantum attack.

These projects can align with best practices detailed in global standards and frameworks as they apply to most projects, most of the time and they are generally accepted as best practices. However, some organizations face barriers to adopting quantum technologies.

Microlearning

There is more online content about quantum project and program management.

- What does the technical stack look like in your organization?
- What type of projects do you see in your industry and are they outlined as a program of projects (Figure 1.2)?
- What quantum technology project management services are available?
- What quantum technology projects are underway in your supply chain?

CHAPTER 5

Quantum Imperatives and Barriers

> *"In the best case, organizations that begin to assess their quantum-readiness now will have time to migrate their most important systems to use quantum-resistant cryptography before threat actors (and business competitors) obtain quantum computers."*
> Canadian Forum for Digital Infrastructure Resilience 2024, 6

Organizations and governments are urged to start their quantum journey (Figure 1.2) and especially to secure their systems and data against quantum cybersecurity threats. There is global consensus among quantum technology thought leaders (some already cited like the World Economic Forum and Michele Mosca) to *prioritize* post-quantum cryptographic migrations and quantum technology projects and promptly begin their quantum journeys.

Start Now Imperative

There are many imperatives to begin the journey toward quantum technologies (the case for change) and can be grouped into seven broad categories:

1. **Operational necessity:** It is widely agreed that Shor's algorithm has the potential to break previously intractable encryption when paired with a powerful and stable enough quantum computer (Q-Day risk). Therefore, organizations that currently rely on common classical encryption (e.g., RSA-2048) will need to transition to post-quantum resistant solutions (e.g., NIST Kyber and Dilithium)

or risk the security of their systems and sensitive data. Some organizations may be required by regulations to migrate to quantum-resistant solutions.

2. **Project criticality:** Even though the risk of a cryptographically-relevant quantum computer breaking an organization's current encryption (e.g., decryption) may be in the future, there is a risk today that an organization's most sensitive data (e.g., "crown jewels") could be stolen and decrypted later with a quantum computer ("steal now, decrypt later" risk). Therefore, it is critical to protect current systems and data today with a minimum viable cybersecurity foundation that has the capabilities to extend protection, detection, and recovery capabilities for emerging technologies like quantum computing.

3. **Program complexity:** Many experts caution that implementing new cryptography like post-quantum algorithms from NIST "can be extremely disruptive and often takes decades to complete" (NIST 2021, 2). And "migrating an organization's cryptographic systems to PQC will require significant effort. Organizations should begin planning now given that the effort and time needed (e.g., to investigate, analyze, plan, procure, migrate and validate new PQC) will not be small and it will be different for every organization"[25] (Canadian Forum for Digital Infrastructure Resilience 2024, 4). However, the project duration is often vendor-dependent, and vendors can be extremely innovative with their design approaches! Program and project management are precisely designed to manage project criticality and complexity, reduce risk, and deliver the required quality.

4. **Quantum opportunities:** Quantum computing offers many capabilities like simulation and optimization that are attractive to innovators and disruptors. These promising capabilities lure organizations toward quantum computing and other quantum

---

[25]Our book *Quantum Cybersecurity Program Management* (Skulmoski and Memari 2025a) was written precisely to address these challenges with a risk-based approach organizations can apply and tailor to their program of quantum technology projects and initiatives.

technologies (e.g., QKD and quantum computing applied to autonomous vehicle traffic management).

5. **Strategic priority:** Most G20 countries (e.g., the United States, Canada, Australia, and the Netherlands) and other forward-looking nations have identified quantum technologies as a strategic priority with goals to adopt and expand their nation's capabilities. For example, "Make Canada a world leader in the continued development, deployment and use of quantum computing hardware and software—to the benefit of Canadian industry, governments and citizens" (Government of Canada 2022, 5). Or "The *National Quantum Strategy* recognizes the importance of commercialization opportunities, robust infrastructure, a skilled workforce, clear standards and (most importantly) community trust to the long-term success of quantum in Australia" (Department of Industry, Science and Resources 2023, 4). Given the importance of quantum technologies to nations, organizations may benefit from government programs to assist with quantum technologies adoption.

6. **Public-key encryption deprecation:** NIST is leading the migration to PQC, setting a 2030 deadline to phase out (deprecate) RSA-2048 and ECC-256 encryption, with a full ban (disallow) by 2035. This transition addresses quantum computing threats, including "harvest now, decrypt later" attacks, by prioritizing quantum-resistant encryption. It is an operational necessity to transition to quantum-secure encryption to prevent compliance and legal risks.

7. **Executive's personal liability:** Some jurisdictions extend compliance risks to company officers, executives, and directors, as they may be personally accountable to implement sufficient cybersecurity. For instance, the *General Data Protection Regulation* in the European Union and the *Caremark Doctrine* in the United States have been successfully applied to hold leadership personally responsible for cybersecurity incidents. There are potential board member and executive liabilities here for some leadership roles.

Therefore, for a variety of imperatives, organizations are encouraged to begin their quantum journey by implementing a program of projects and initiatives guided by the "right" amount of technical maturity.

> ## Microlearning
>
> There is a growing body of quantum-related information online to explore about the imperatives of a quick start.
>
> - Learn what the key drivers (imperatives) in your industry to adopt quantum technologies,
> - Find out if there are government agencies with quantum awareness resources that can be used in your awareness initiatives,
> - Are there any legal or regulator imperatives?

Barriers to Adopting Quantum Technologies

Technology adoption by individuals, organizations, and societies is the process to use new technologies and often to improve efficiency and effectiveness. Technology adoption has become a continuous process as new technologies emerge like QML. Despite the promise of innovation or the risk of quantum threats and widespread encouragement to start a quantum journey without delay, there are many persistent adoption barriers[26] including:

1. **Lagging regulatory frameworks:** Organizations may delay their quantum journey until the regulatory environment(s) in their industry mature. However, introduce the basics of ADKar to guide the stakeholders to quantum technologies while the regulatory details emerge (e.g., quantum computing awareness campaigns and

---

[26]In 2024 and 2025, Greg Skulmoski addressed professional audiences (e.g., project managers, supply chain professionals, lawyers) and polled whether their organizations had a quantum strategy. In total, 93 percent of the respondents ($n = 371$) indicated their organization did not have a strategy nor were they implementing quantum technology project (e.g., awareness and cryptographic agility). This research suggests that despite the urgings of leading experts and governments, many organizations may not be far along their journeys at the time of this publication.

experimentation with quantum algorithms can occur while regulatory frameworks unfold). Look for regulatory compliance solutions that address today's and tomorrow's requirements for post-quantum cryptographic migrations and cryptographic agility.

2. **Quantum obliviousness:** Some organizations may not be following quantum developments and therefore might not be aware of the dual potentialities of quantum technologies and the steady progress toward a cryptographically-relevant quantum computer. Again, address any quantum unfamiliarity with ADKar awareness initiatives.

3. **Lack of quantum competencies:** Organizations may delay initiating quantum technology projects if they lack competent people. Competence is knowledge, skills, and experience that are effectively applied to the benefit of the organization (Skulmoski and Hartman 2010; Figure 5.1). Some researchers also include motives (e.g., the achievement motive) and traits (e.g., being an early adopter of technology at home and at work). There is a global shortage of people with competencies related to quantum technologies.

   There are many ways to increase quantum technology competence such as through training and experimentation, university classes in quantum mechanics, partnering with external quantum SMEs, funding scholarships to recruit future employees, joining a quantum technologies community of practice, mentoring, self-directed learning and reading (e.g., this book), and so on. Related to competence is the stakeholder's personal situation like age or health that may impact their desire to engage and learn. Personal misalignment may reduce the desire to genuinely engage in a program of projects (e.g., the stakeholder is 14 months away from leaving the organization and starting their retirement).

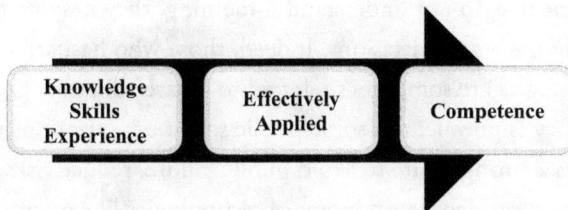

Figure 5.1 Competence model

4. **Immature quantum industry:** The quantum technologies industry may be categorized in its early growth phase with considerable technology risk and uncertainty. Early stage technologies are susceptible to many risks and change. Therefore, some organizations avoid early adopter behaviors and let technologies like quantum computing mature before their adoption.

5. **Emerging data privacy and security environment:** As the quantum industry matures, so is data privacy and the security environment as they pertain to quantum technologies. However, there is considerable global effort and resources to guide organizations to reduce data privacy and security risks such as the NIST (2020) Privacy Framework that is freely available and translated into multiple languages. Organizations have departmental SMEs (e.g., compliance, risk and legal units) that monitor regulations impacting their business operations. These people can also add to their lists to monitor data privacy and security developments and risks related to quantum technologies.

6. **Weak Cross-Industry Engagement:** Some organizations compete while others also collaborate. Since the quantum industry and its technologies are emerging, collaboration opportunities are not always readily available and advertised that may inhibit adoption. However, competition is often the standard operating procedure rather than collaboration for many organizations. Both approaches yield healthy results when applied at the right time; however, strategic collaborations in quantum technologies can be mutually beneficial for collaborating parties.

7. **Quantum Hesitancy:** Like waiting for regulations or quantum technologies to mature, quantum hesitancy is indecision and delay to update strategies and adopt quantum technologies. It is natural when people do not understand something, they hesitate to avoid making the wrong decisions. Indeed, those who hesitate with new technologies are sometimes referred to as late adopters. Quantum hesitancy is prevalent in some public sector organizations where there is a strong desire to avoid public failure, reduce risks, and instead be a prudent late adopter of technologies like quantum computing. Treat quantum hesitancy with quantum awareness strategies

especially for risks related to the arrival of a cryptographically-relevant quantum computer.

8. **Financial:** Adopting technologies like PQC takes time and money that may be in short supply resulting in an adoption barrier. However, there are many front-end activities like experimenting with quantum algorithms and developing use cases that are relatively less expensive and can add significant value when there is approval to proceed with quantum technology projects.

9. **Near-term focus:** Some organizations are focused on near-term projects like implementing AI and zero trust technologies. This is often due to the demand for technology projects (e.g., discovery inventories and post-quantum cryptographic migrations) exceeding the supply of resources and higher priority projects are initiated. The result is a delay in initiating the quantum program of projects that may lead the organization to rely upon compressed schedule strategies to catch up.

These are the major quantum technology barriers facing organizations. These barriers may be combined, such as quantum technologies are not being implemented today due to a near-term focus and the lack of financial resources. To better understand the barriers to quantum technologies adoption the reader is invited to use and tailor the Quantum Technology Barriers to Adoption Gizmo to help their analysis (Table 5.1). Add any additional barriers as required.

Like other Gizmos, the purpose is not to arrive at a score for each question but rather to guide discussion (e.g., "why is there a wide variety of responses?") and help lead to a shared understanding of the organization and departments' barriers to adopting quantum technologies. Conclude the discussion with problem-solving and follow-up actions.

Some organizations have not begun their quantum program of projects due to adoption barriers like quantum hesitancy. As a result, they may need to break through barriers to adopt quantum technologies that is discussed in the next chapter.

To sum up, most organizations face barriers to implementing new technologies if only due to financial barriers. Implementing quantum technologies and breaking through barriers can benefit from a diverse

Table 5.1 Quantum technology barriers to adoption Gizmo

Quantum technology adoption barriers	Rate, discuss, and act	Barrier effect High Low
1. Lagging Regulatory Frameworks	To what degree if any, do lagging quantum regulations have on our business operations?	5 – 4 – 3 – 2 – 1
2. Quantum Obliviousness	How much quantum oblivion is there in our organization or department?	5 – 4 – 3 – 2 – 1
3. Lack of Quantum Competencies	How competent are the people in our department or organization with quantum technologies?	5 – 4 – 3 – 2 – 1
4. Immature Quantum Industry	How mature is the quantum industry in our line of work?	5 – 4 – 3 – 2 – 1
5. Emerging Data Privacy and Security Environment	How developed is the quantum data privacy and security environment for our industry?	5 – 4 – 3 – 2 – 1
6. Weak Cross-Industry Engagement	How engaged with each other is our industry regarding quantum technologies?	5 – 4 – 3 – 2 – 1
7. Quantum Hesitancy	How hesitant are the people in our department or organization and partners about adopting quantum technologies?	5 – 4 – 3 – 2 – 1
8. Financial	To what degree do the costs present a barrier to adopting quantum technologies?	5 – 4 – 3 – 2 – 1
9. Near-Term Focus	To what degree is the organization focused on near-term projects rather than adopting quantum technologies?	5 – 4 – 3 – 2 – 1

body of knowledge and competence drawing from marketing and sales, leadership mentoring, and project and product management disciplines. Bringing quantum technologies into organizations is a sustained exercise in organizational change management where the reader is invited to apply, tailor, and combine their favorite approaches with those detailed in this book.

Microlearning

Barriers to technology adoption have existed for centuries like the first automobiles that were expensive, and the existing roads (infrastructure) were built for horses rather than automobiles. Quantum technologies face similar barriers to adoption like being expensive with an immature infrastructure.

- What enablers of technology are successful in your industry and discipline?
- What quantum-related regulations apply to your industry and discipline?
- Is your organization and industry traditionally late or early adopters of innovations and technologies?
- Are data privacy and security rules and regulations changing in your industry due to quantum technologies?

CHAPTER 6

Breaking Through Quantum Barriers

> *Change is a threat when done to me, but an opportunity when done by me.*
>
> Rosabeth Moss Kanter

Rosabeth Moss Kanter (1983) published her influential book *The Change Masters* and presented the principles of successful organizational change management like following a collaborative change management process with supportive and engaged leadership. A half century later, the change management discipline is mature, and quantum stakeholders can learn from their best practices including breaking through barriers to adopting quantum technologies.

Introduction to Organizational Change Management Theory

Organizational change management is an approach to ensure planned changes to the organization are predictable and sustainable. Organizations make changes for many reasons like innovating with quantum computing to stay competitive or provide optimized products and services. Organizations also change for survival like strengthening their cryptographic ecosystem with PQC and mitigating the quantum threat. Change occurs to comply with new regulatory requirements (e.g., privacy or reporting). While there are many reasons for organizational change management, most can be managed through a formal change management approach.

Organizational change management differs from project change management where organizational change management includes three phases: pre-project, project, and post-project activities (Figure 1.1). Notice that the project is the middle phase of change management where project deliverables are provided to the change manager (project sponsor) to use post-project.

The project change management process differs from the organizational change management process. Project managers use the project change management process to make changes to elements in the approved plan. For example, the project manager may raise a change request and follow the project change management process to re-baseline the approved schedule.[27] Both organizational change management and project change management include processes to reduce risks and increase the probability of a successful change. These processes can be optimized ahead of quantum technology projects (Figure 1.2). The project sponsor is responsible for organizational change management and the project manager is responsible for project change management.

There are many change management methods, tools, and frameworks that have evolved in the last 50 years. The *Standard for Change Management* details the change management process (Figure 6.1). Their change management process is typical: strategize, plan, execute, evaluate, and close out. Change management in this book aligns with these foundational standards and frameworks (Table 4.1) that represent generally accepted best practices.

Since the change management process to implement the program of projects (Figure 1.2) will likely be a decade or more, program and project closure are out of scope for this book (but a mini-change management close out process may take place for a short-term plan like a 100-day quantum awareness plan. In *Cybersecurity Project Management* (Skulmoski 2022), we provide an overview of the *project* close out process and in *Quantum Cybersecurity*, we provide an overview of the *program* close out process.

---

[27]In *Cybersecurity Project Management* (Skulmoski 2022), we detail the integration of project change management with a project risk management approach that can be used on quantum technologies projects to reduce risks.

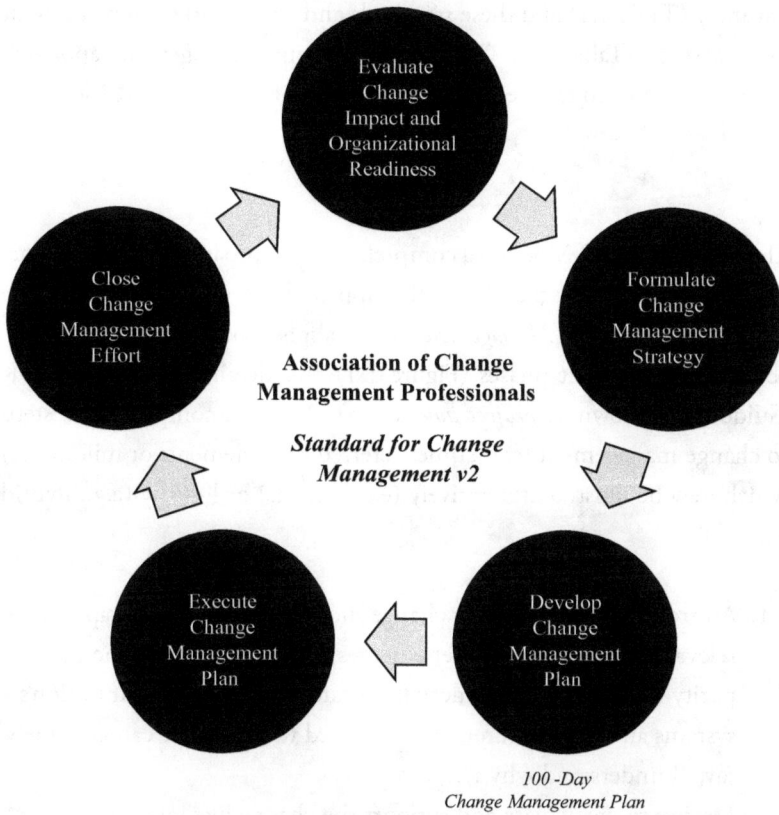

Figure 6.1 ACMP change management process

The value proposition of the ACMP change management process (and any other best practices represented in standards and frameworks is "follow me to minimize risks and achieve the required amount of quality." Generally, following lean processes reduces risks. The ACMP change management process is iterative and aligns with the Deming Cycle for quality management (plan, do, check, and act). Iterative quality management is the basis for change management, agile project management (sprints), continual improvement, and other "best practices."

The point is many of these management theories, standards, and frameworks incorporate quality and risk management best practices like gap analysis, strategy and plan development, implementation, monitoring, and continual improvement. Since risk and quality management are common elements, applying and combining best practices can occur naturally (Table 4.1) and these standards and frameworks can be thought of as a stack (Table 3.2). The popular change management approach loosely applied and tailored in this book is the Prosci ADKAR Model.

ADKar

The Prosci ADKAR Model is a comprehensive approach to organizational change management that "fits" the approach in *Accelerated Quantum Technologies Change Management* as it aligns with pre-project, project, and post-project phases (Figure 1.1) and detailed in the PMBOK Guide (also known as *project boundaries*). ADKAR comprises five steps to change management (sometimes referred to as elements or milestones) which may be illustrated iteratively (e.g., sprints) or linearly (e.g., hybrid waterfall):

1. **Awareness:** of the need for change such as when a cryptographically-relevant quantum computer emerges, it is likely to have the capacity to break classical encryption safeguarding the organization's systems and data. Awareness is achieved when people can genuinely say, "I understand why ...,"
2. **Desire:** to participate and support the change like joining the post-quantum cryptographic migration project team or a community of practice. Desire is achieved when people genuinely say, "I have decided to participate ...,"
3. **Knowledge:** on how to change and implement quantum technologies such as using schedule compression techniques to accelerate the post-quantum cryptographic migrations. Knowledge is sufficient when people say, "I have a good idea how to ...,"
4. **Ability:** to implement the change (e.g., a project to plan, migrate, and validate the transition to PQC). Ability is achieved when people say, "I am able to ...,"
5. **Reinforcement:** to sustain the change such as updating procurement policies to restrict purchasing quantum-vulnerable technologies. Reinforcement is successful when people say, "I will continue to participate ...."

While awareness, knowledge, and desire (ADKar) appear as sequential steps, awareness and desire can occur in quick succession,[28] leading to a thirst for knowledge. Therefore, the path through ADKar varies as it is a personal journey.

The focus of the ADKar approach in this book is on engaging people in the organization to become aware of the change (e.g., quantum technologies), desire the change, and develop a deeper knowledge of the change. In addition, the Prosci ADKAR change management approach includes extensive tools, processes, and an accreditation pathway for learners such as those applying change management to quantum technology projects. Therefore, using their high-level framework reduces the need for many readers to learn new things when change management involving quantum technologies is framed within the Prosci ADKAR framework and aligned with other commonly used frameworks and standards (Table 4.1).

Awareness

While a change management strategy and plan are being developed, spread awareness and the case for change. Awareness is the goal and the intended outcome in this phase. Awareness is enhanced when the following questions can be *answered* and tuned for quantum computing:

1. What is the scope of the change? *Plan, implement, and optimize quantum computing to improve manufacturing operations,*
2. Why quantum computing? Why now? *Quantum computing can optimize manufacturing throughput and maximize the mean time between maintenance cycles giving our company a competitive advantage,*
3. What if we don't implement these changes? *Our competitors are likely to reduce manufacturing costs resulting in a loss of our market share.*

---

[28]Think about being on a long-distance flight and you find your favorite film is available (awareness) and then you plan to watch it (desire) during the inflight supper. Awareness occurred and desire quickly followed without any effort.

Since there are dual potentialities for quantum technologies, tailor the awareness questions and answers for quantum threats and add them to the change management communications plan:

1. What is the scope of the change? *Plan, migrate, and validate the transition to NIST-approved post-quantum cryptography (NIST SPHINCS+),*

2. Why migrate to new cryptography? Why now? *A cryptographically-relevant quantum computer used by a hacker will be able to access and steal our data and disrupt our systems unless our organization migrates to quantum-safe cryptography. The migration away from classical cryptography (2048-RSA) and adoption of quantum-safe cryptography may take a decade and therefore, it is crucial to start now. Plus, the 2048-RSA encryption we use will be deprecated in 2030 and disallowed in 2035. We need your help.*

3. What if we don't implement these changes? *If our systems and data are compromised by a hacker with a cryptographically-relevant quantum computer, our customers may lose trust in our services, and we may lose significant market share.*

Therefore, an early series of projects and initiatives in the quantum technologies program is to develop awareness, enthusiasm, and desire (e.g., sustainable funding). Given the criticality and complexity of the quantum program, we recommend to formally initiate awareness projects.

The initial awareness goals include setting up the quantum transition team, estimating the scope of the quantum program of projects (e.g., Figure 4.1) including rough order of magnitude estimates for the budget and schedule timelines and engaging stakeholders. The quantum champion might collaborate with other like-minded colleagues to assist with subsequent quantum technology projects and change management. For a major and sustained change management program like quantum technology adoption, it is critical to get the support of the executive leaders in the organization like the chief executive officer.

Change Management Stakeholders

The reader may find there are equally enthusiastic people in their organization willing to join the quantum transition team, through to people who have never heard about quantum technologies, let alone the existential risk a cryptographically-relevant quantum computer may present to the organization (Table 6.1)

Table 6.1 **Quantum stakeholders**

Role	Responsibility
Executive leadership and board members	Support, sponsor, and maintain the momentum toward quantum program targets like post-quantum cryptographic migrations.
Quantum technologies sponsor	Typically, the sponsor is the manager for a group of end users of the new technologies (e.g., the manufacturing manager).
Quantum champions	Champions spread awareness and contribute to perhaps a decade of quantum technology projects; they may be found anywhere in the organization and may have a formal or informal champion role.
Quantum project manager	The project manager oversees all or parts of the program of projects like spreading awareness for quantum technologies in the organization.
Quantum subject matter experts (SMEs)	Quantum technologies SMEs engage throughout the technology life cycle (Figure 1.1). For instance, they may specialize in quantum technologies hardware performance tuning or quantum machine learning.
Cybersecurity SMEs	These SMEs specialize in the quantum cybersecurity functions of govern, identify, protect, detect, respond, and recover as outlined in the NIST Cybersecurity Framework.
IT SMEs	There are many supporting technology SMEs like an infrastructure engineer or a database administrator.
Supporting SMEs	There are nontechnical SMEs found in quantum technologies procurement, legal and compliance, recruiting, training, and others support roles.
External stakeholders	Partners, vendors, third party, clients and customers, consultants, regulatory agencies, and others may also collaborate.
Quantum technology end users	Quantum technologies end users (e.g., in manufacturing) use the technologies delivered by project teams.

Also look for non-traditional collaborators in your organization like marketing experts who can advise on how to get and keep your stakeholder's attention to achieve your quantum technology change management goals. These experts may be other managers who have a successful record of business case approvals. The quantum technologies team will often begin with just one person but can expand and include people throughout the organization.

There are likely other specialized quantum roles that may benefit organizations. Indeed, a person may find themselves in multiple roles (e.g., quantum champion and project manager). Begin quantum awareness initiatives and projects with these stakeholders and tailor as required.

Prioritize Leadership Awareness

A goal of quantum awareness is to secure sustained executive support, engagement, and resource commitment if it is not already achieved. Executive leadership support allows the quantum transition team to proceed with resources and approval to begin their quantum journey. Simply, strong leadership support results in reduced resistance to change and therefore is a critical success factor for change management.

There are early awareness actions (adapted from the World Economic Forum 2022, 21–22) for leadership including board members, cybersecurity leadership, and steering committees (Tables 6.2 and 6.3). Cybersecurity leadership, if they have not already done so, can also accelerate awareness about quantum technologies and the distinct actions they can take (Table 6.3). Quantum awareness campaigns and mentoring by a quantum champion (guided by Tables 6.2 and 6.3) can expedite quantum awareness, enthusiasm, desire, and commitment.

Quantum awareness is facilitated by aligning to standards (e.g., PMBOK Guide) and frameworks (e.g., NIST Cybersecurity Framework and ITIL Service Management) since they provide common terminology, tools, processes, and theory, all of which provide the opportunity for a shared understanding. Indeed, these standards and frameworks are globally adopted. Therefore, we endeavor to align with terminology in de facto global standards and frameworks in our approach to quantum technologies change management.

Table 6.2 Awareness recommendations for leadership

Learn about ...	Take action ...
• the dual potentialities of quantum technologies and their impacts on businesses, • the legal and regulatory implications of quantum technologies, • the risk treatment options like post-quantum cryptography, • the best practices to manage organizational change (e.g., Prosci ADKAR method) and best practices in project and technology service management (e.g., ITIL).	• to establish a minimum viable cybersecurity foundation if not already achieved to protect against the "steal now, decrypt later" risk, • to develop a holistic approach (people, processes, and technologies) to adopt quantum technologies and balance protection from quantum risks, with organizational agility, • to invest in updating and replacing susceptible with resistant post-quantum cryptographic systems, • to prioritize and include cryptographic agility in procurement practices, • to hire and train knowledgeable staff in both the IT and end user departments, • to coordinate both internally and externally to develop a program plan to transition to quantum technologies.

Table 6.3 Awareness recommendations for cybersecurity leadership

Learn about ...	Take action ...
• relevant government regulations and industry accreditations, • quantum technologies milestones including when a cryptographically-relevant quantum computer becomes available and powerful enough to break classical cryptography (e.g., the "Z" parameter in Mosca's Theorem), • others in your organization who are keen to be quantum early adopters and future collaborators or have a special interest in managing privacy risks.	• to spread awareness up, down, inside, and outside of your organization to leverage quantum opportunities and to implement post-quantum cryptographic-resistant risk treatment projects, • to conduct quantum-related risk analyses (both positive and negative risks), • to plan and implement a cryptographic inventory followed by risk analysis, prioritization, and treatment (Figure 4.2).

Developing awareness may also include training that has its own distinct discipline: andragogy—the practice and methods of teaching adults. In this book, we apply formal training methods like the ADDIE Model of Instructional Design (Figure 6.2) to raise and extend awareness. For example, the ADDIE Model of Instructional Design begins when an

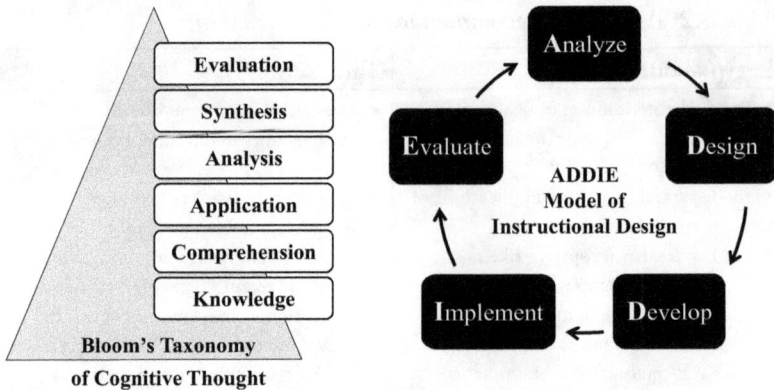

Figure 6.2 Andragogy—Adult training and learning foundation

instructional designer *analyses* training and awareness requirements and *designs*, *develops*, and *implements* awareness and training projects, followed by training and learning *evaluation* of quantum technologies awareness.[29]

Bloom's Taxonomy of Cognitive Thought (e.g., how learning progresses from simple to complex thought) guides awareness curriculum development (Figure 6.2). Organizations can first provide introductory knowledge about quantum technologies, use cases, and cybersecurity to orient the learner. To innovate and protect with quantum technologies, many of the organization's people will need to proceed through Bloom's Taxonomy levels beginning with basic knowledge and comprehension of quantum technologies. They can progress to higher levels of understanding quantum technologies through additional training, experimentation, and mentoring to develop quantum technology use cases.

Organizations can benefit from a formal upskilling approach to prepare for adoption and optimization of quantum computing technologies and use cases because these frameworks guide teams to deliver while minimizing risks and providing the required level of quality. We direct the reader to *Cybersecurity Training: A Pathway to Readiness* (Skulmoski and Walker 2023) to learn about a project-oriented approach to technology

---

[29]Notice the Deming quality cycle (plan–do–check–act) underlies the ADDIE Model of Instructional Design! This is part of the reason that standards and frameworks can be stacked.

training and awareness including recommendations to establish quantum communities of practice and other techniques to progress change and engagement.

Awareness Error Messages

The number one error message from stakeholders related to lack of awareness is repeatedly asking the same question. For instance, if people ask, "Why do we need quantum technologies; we are doing fine now?" this question illuminates the lack of awareness for the dual potentialities of technologies. Therefore, update messaging to better explain the severe risks related to the dual potentialities of quantum technologies. Close awareness gaps with additional messaging and feedback opportunities with executive leadership including the CEO to explain the necessity of the quantum journey and the risks of delay.

Microlearning

The awareness phase of ADKar kicks off the quantum journey and is enhanced with online resources:

- What quantum resources are available in your industry to support quantum awareness?
- How can RACI charts be used to manage and collaborate with your quantum stakeholders?

Desire

Awareness of quantum technologies is necessary but not sufficient for progress; there needs to be the desire to plan, implement, and adopt quantum technologies. Desire is a goal and the intended outcome in this phase: a genuine willingness to support and engage in a program of quantum technologies. Creating desire for change can be the most challenging aspect of change management and the key question to answer is, "What's in it for me?" Therefore, regularly inform your stakeholders why quantum technologies are beneficial for them since it is a critical success factor and is part of the ADKar communications messaging.

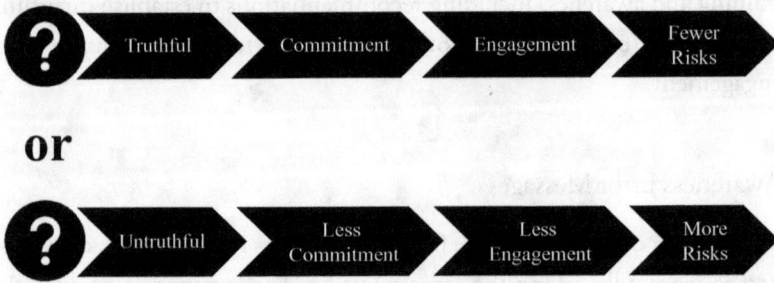

Figure 6.3 Truth telling, commitment, engagement, and risk

Desire can be instantly created after the "right" awareness message with an immediate desire for more information about quantum technologies (adKar phase). Desire is related to commitment, which is also necessary to progress through the ADKar phases.

Commitment

Commitment is a transparent and reciprocal agreement between the organization and the individual to achieve their change management goals. It is also known as buy-in that varies from high to low buy-in (Hubbart 2023). The project champion will strive to create commitment up and down the organization chart.

A key part of getting and maintaining commitment is truth telling and trust. If trust is damaged by falsehoods or misrepresentations, it will be difficult to achieve buy-in (Figure 6.3). Truth telling is a best practice in crisis management (e.g., a ransomware attack) and is also used to remove quantum technology adoption barriers.

Therefore, truth telling messages are built into change management communications to develop and maintain commitment, foster engagement, and reduce risks. Schedule senior leadership and quantum project sponsors for regular feedback and cocreation opportunities based on open, truthful, reciprocal, and empathetic conversations with quantum stakeholders to build and sustain trust and change momentum.

While the Prosci ADKAR method emphasizes building and sustaining desire, commitment is also important to change success (Figure 6.4).

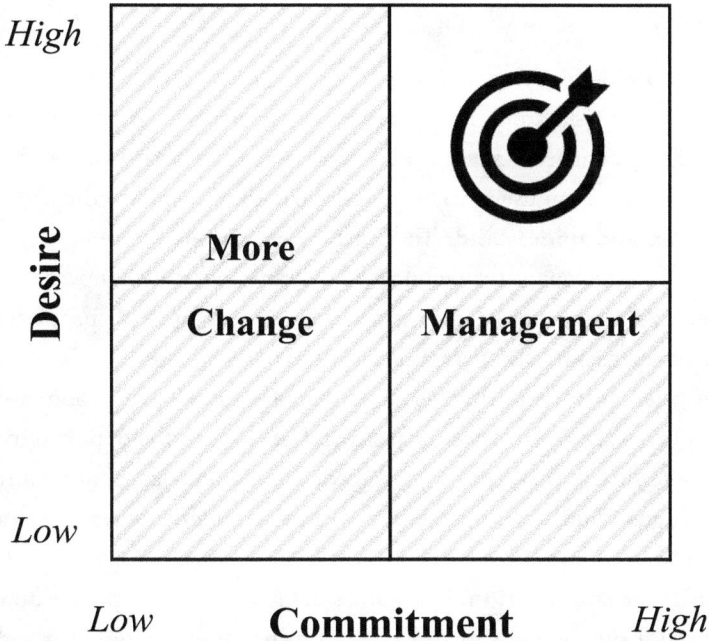

High

Desire

More Change   **Management**

Low

Low   **Commitment**   *High*

Figure 6.4 Change management desire and commitment matrix

One may have a high desire, but with low commitment, action may lag. For instance, one can desire to be fit and perhaps lose 4 kg, but it is the commitment to eat healthy foods most of the time and exercise regularly that brings one closer to their fitness goals. Desire alone may not be enough; therefore, both high (sufficient) commitment and desire for the quantum journey needs to be developed and sustained. While desire is critical, it is people completing their quantum project work on time (desire and commitment) that allows the program of quantum technology projects to progress.

Desire and commitment[30] differ with each stakeholder necessitating almost an individual approach for each to progress through the ADKar phases and to address any resistance to change (e.g., quantum technology adoption barriers).

---

[30]Hereafter, when we use desire, we mean desire including commitment. We avoid using "desire and commitment" for brevity.

Risk of Resistance to Change

In the ADKAR model, desire may be hampered by resistance to change. Many ADKar risks are related to resistance to change (quantum technology adoption barriers are addressed later). There are best practices quantum champions can use to manage resistance to change including:

Listen and understand: There are many reasons for being hesitant about adopting quantum technologies; terminology like superposition and entanglement can be confusing. When engaging with people who share concerns first listen to fully understand and use techniques like active listening to confirm there is a shared understanding. Sometimes people just want their concerns heard and once given the opportunity to provide feedback, they can progress toward a genuine desire for quantum technologies. Find out if there is a root cause or underlying reasons to any resistance to change.

Shift the conversation: Sometimes desire lags because people do not understand the methods or processes to bring about change (e.g., what is the process to complete post-quantum cryptographic migrations?). Instead, focus on the rationale or need for change (e.g., data and systems are at risk unless organizations migrate to the new PQC) and *park* the "how" to be addressed for later in the ADKar process if the details are unavailable (e.g., provide details of post-quantum cryptographic migration during the Knowledge phase and elaborated in the design phase of the project).

Provide pathways: Identify the choices for employees and the consequences of the different pathways (engage in the quantum journey or resist). An influencer like a manager or respected SME can sometimes help the hesitant person to work through their barriers to adoption. Do not underestimate the impact of personal appeals to join the quantum journey.

Provide hope and the quantum vision: Sometimes it only takes a clear vision of the organization's target state, and the innovative opportunities quantum computing can provide to develop desire. The quantum vision and goals are elaborated in the business strategy and crafted into a communications plan that *sell* the quantum vision. To create desire in the quantum stakeholders and to break through any barriers, prepare answers for the different stakeholders (Table 6.1) to the question: "What's in it for me?"

Therefore, take a proactive approach to prevent and mitigate resistance to quantum technologies. Some organizations have successfully addressed resistance to change by providing change management training opportunities to leadership and supervisors early in the quantum technologies journey. Managers with change management knowledge, tools, and processes can support others to join the quantum journey and engage in its projects.

Knowledge

Following desire and committing to be part of the change, the next step of ADKar change management is to develop knowledge of how to adopt quantum technologies (e.g., a program of projects, Figure 4.1). Developing sufficient knowledge is a goal and the intended outcome in this phase. Stakeholders may also want to know what new quantum competencies (e.g., knowledge and skills) are required. The early quantum technologies require specialized competencies like engineering and software development. However, later versions of quantum technologies will be more user-friendly with the feel of a desktop application (e.g., chemistry workflows).

Stakeholders (Table 6.1) may also want information about any changes to work processes, roles, and responsibilities due to adopting quantum technologies. Share information about the two phases of change that can affect stakeholders: (i) the transition to quantum technologies and then (ii) working in a digital ecosystem combined with quantum and classical computing technologies. Provide information to stakeholders about what happens in the transition to quantum technologies and what happens in the target state. Stakeholders will still use classical computing in the foreseeable future for low computational tasks like sending an email or requesting vacation from their employer. Add this is the type of information to the quantum technologies communications plan presented later in this book.

Employees may worry whether they can succeed in the future with quantum technologies. Therefore, share the organization's plans to prepare them for their quantum journey. Simplify the vision of the quantum future into using new hardware and software as done before by employees in the organization. They will continue to be supported by the organization with ITIL's Incident Management practice to manage any incidents with quantum technologies.

Of considerable importance at the front-end of the quantum technology program of projects is to consider the degree to which the project schedule needs to be accelerated if any. Schedule compression (discussed later) is a critical strategic decision and therefore this knowledge component of ADKar is considered early during quantum strategy development. Specifically, should there be a significant compressed schedule target state-ability gap, then the gap should be closed for the compressed schedule strategy to be effective, or a different strategy other than compressed schedule needs to be considered. That is, do not use a compressed schedule strategy if the project team and organization are weak with this risky and complex project execution technique; determine whether schedule compression is appropriate sooner rather than later.

Facilitating knowledge acquisition is an upskilling exercise that varies along a training and education continuum. For example, there may be simple quantum technology awareness sessions through to educational opportunities to earn a degree in a quantum technologies field.

Microlearning

There are many ways to develop knowledge and to upskill like reading books (thank you!). Find more online about developing knowledge for the quantum journey of projects:

- What training and mentoring resources are available online and in your organization?
- Are there quantum technologies communities of practice in your discipline?
- Can you find gamification resources (e.g., leaderboards and serious games like scenario simulations) to support the ADKar phase of the quantum technologies journey? Gamification techniques can increase engagement and learning.
- Find out why successful adult educators use andragogy rather than pedagogy to provide successful training and learning.

Ability

In the Prosci ADKAR Model, the ability step is the person or organization using awareness, desire, and knowledge to create change. In our book, ability is the quantum technology deliverables (e.g., PQC) provided through a project delivery approach (e.g., agile). In *Shields Up: Cybersecurity Project Management* (Skulmoski 2022), we detailed project management best practices. In *Quantum Cybersecurity Program Management,* we detailed how to plan, implement, and optimize a program of projects. These two books guide readers to provide a lean approach to implement projects and programs (adkAr) including quantum technologies.

Reinforcement

At the end of the project life cycle, the deliverables are provided to IT operations and the project sponsor to manage. Quantum technologies can change processes, roles, and responsibilities that require new competencies. Change management leaders reinforce stakeholder adoption of quantum technologies. Monitor the ADKAR status and use governance best practices to successfully deliver quantum technologies. Identify any resistance and help them on their quantum journey. Continue

---

Microlearning

There are many ADKAR resources, and some can be applied and tailored to the ADKar phase for quantum technologies; find out about:

- ADKAR use cases (successful and unsuccessful examples),
- ADKAR terminology that is commonly used throughout the Prosci approach to change management,
- How to facilitate individual change,
- The Prosci structured approach to change management and their workshop tools to progress through the quantum technologies change management ADKar phases,
- How do measure ADKAR change management progress,
- Tools to equip senior leadership for leading change.

Table 6.4 ADKar status tracker

Stakeholders	ADKAR status				
	A	D	K	A	R
Executive leadership and board members	G	G	A		
Quantum technologies sponsor	G	G	A		
Quantum champions	G	G	G		
Quantum project manager	G	G	G		
Quantum SMEs	G	G	R	Out of Scope for ADKar	
Cybersecurity SMEs	G	G	R		
IT SMEs	G	G	–		
Supporting SMEs	G	A	–		
External stakeholders	A	–	–		
Quantum technologies end users	G	–	–		

to provide training, mentoring, and support. Continue to nurture sustained leadership and financial support for the program of quantum technology projects. Finally, celebrate success as there is a risk that change management fatigue may occur especially in extended schedule compression projects.

Tracking ADKar Progress

Monitor awareness and the other steps in the ADKar change management process (Table 6.4) according to project stakeholders (more fully discussed later and illustrated in Figures 10.3 and 10.4).

Track ADKar progress with the RAG status (red, amber, and green) approach. Here for example, most stakeholders are progressing according to plan (green status = *G*), but a few are a bit slow (amber status = *A*). Some stakeholders (red status = *R*) are behind schedule and require assistance to get back on track. By monitoring ADKar status, change management leaders can pinpoint where additional support may improve progress.

In summary, change management projects and programs inevitably face barriers like quantum technology hesitancy. While the technologies may be new, technology adoption and change management are well understood. Therefore, quantum technology champions can leverage best practices found in research, standards, and frameworks to accelerate their quantum journey and to break through any quantum barriers.

Microlearning

While quantum technologies are emerging, change management has a long history. Look online for more information:

- How popular is the ADKAR method and certification in your industry and discipline?
- Are there other ADKAR practitioners in your organization?
- Review ITIL's Service Value System to see how projects (also known as the Service Value Chain) relate to the project boundaries seen in Figure 1.1.

CHAPTER 7

Technology Adoption Models

> *It's not the strongest of the species that survive, nor the most intelligent, but the one most responsive to change.*
>
> Charles Darwins

One of the most famous change management models for technology is the Technology Adoption Model (Davis 1989), which can be applied to quantum technologies. The goal is for actual system use (Figure 7.1) by end users (e.g., technology adoption). Davis identified the determinants and moderators of technology adoption including perceived ease of use and perceived usefulness of the adopted technology. Hence, leadership can apply and tailor this model and combine it with other change management approaches as we have done in this book. The simplicity of the Davis model is part of its appeal, and it triggered subsequent research to validate variables and relationships.

The Technology Adoption Model also received criticisms and revision recommendations. Some have critiqued the model as simplistic, and it does not fully explain all instances of technology adoption like post-adoption behavior. Some criticized the model for missing adoption determinants like emotional or behavioral factors like peer influence. Indeed, the critical ADKAR characteristic of desire for change is not explicit in the original Technology Adoption Model. The result was other technology adoption models emerged with the goal to *perfectly* model technology adoption.

The Venkatesh research team (2000) reviewed the many models to adopt technology and their determinants for adoption, with the goal to find or develop the *best* model. While the Venkatesh researchers are widely

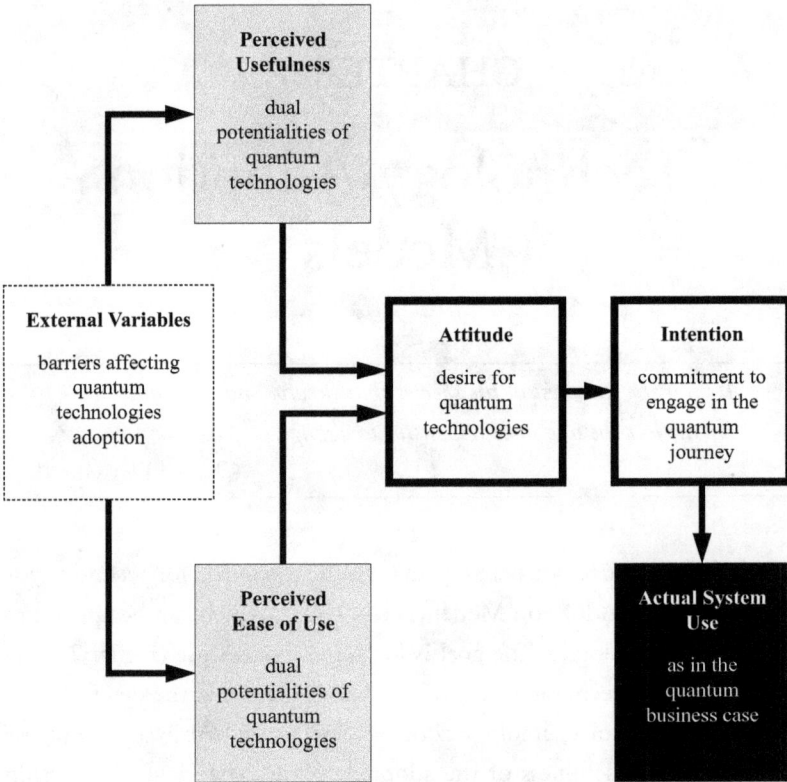

Figure 7.1 Davis Technology Adoption Model tailored for quantum technologies

cited by other researchers for their contributions, our goal in this book is different: identify, apply, tailor, simplify, and combine models (from generally accepted standards and frameworks) that will work *most of the time, for most organizations.* Many in the change management community do not search for the perfect model rather apply one that is close enough, then tailor it to the situation and combine with other models, procedures and so forth as necessary. This is also an agile or adaptive approach—start where you are, with what you have and adapt.

The Venkatesh researchers analyzed 215 studies of technology adoption and identified key determinants of technology adoption that may be applied and tailored to quantum technology adoption and to break through any barriers (Table 7.1). The communications team can use the Quantum Technologies Adoption Determinants to shape messaging through the ADKar phases of change.

Table 7.1 Quantum technologies adoption determinants

Adoption determinants	Communication messaging—*Quantum truths*
Perceived usefulness from quantum technologies	Quantum technology users may not understand quantum technologies' performance and innovation capabilities and hence can benefit from more information. They may also be unaware of the threats posed by a cryptographically-relevant quantum computer.
Perceived ease of use with quantum technologies	Users will likely want to know how difficult it will be for them to use quantum technologies.
Attitude of end users to adopt quantum technologies	The goal is to develop and reinforce positive attitudes toward quantum technologies; negative attitudes are barriers that can be addressed with ADKar techniques.
Social influence of others	Respected and important quantum champions and opinion leaders can influence others to adopt quantum technologies.
Anxiety using quantum technologies	Some people are apprehensive to use new technologies like quantum and hesitate; these users benefit from supports like mentoring from direct managers.
Self-efficacy using quantum technologies	Some are hesitant to use quantum technologies and are more likely to adopt if there are opportunities for support if something goes wrong.
Upskilling opportunities to adopt quantum technologies	Some technology adoption hesitancy is due to lack of skills and can be addressed with learning and supportive opportunities (e.g., quantum a community of practice and time with a quantum mentor).

These common technology adoption determinants (also known as enablers) can be simplified for quantum technologies change management planning purposes (Figure 7.2). While the determinants of technology adoption relationships may be more complex for some organizations, a simple model may be enough to identify common technology adoption determinants and any related barriers. When enough determinants are satisfied for quantum technologies adoption, then sufficient desire and commitment aid progress toward quantum technologies adoption.

There are other moderating influences that may affect technology adoption like the person's age, experience, and gender that can be considered to better understand the quantum technology determinants for the organization. Venkatesh's paper (2003) provides a detailed illustration of the interactions among the technology adoption determinants should

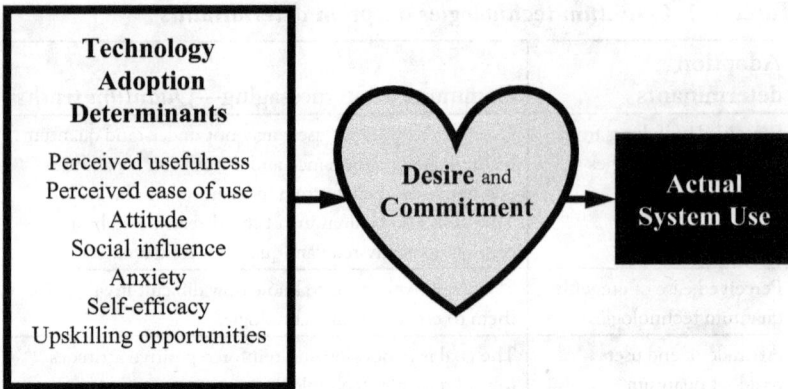

Figure 7.2 Common technology adoption determinants

the reader wish to move beyond our simple depiction of technologies adoption (Figure 7.2).

Later, Ali and his research team (2021) combined the Davis Technology Adoption Model with ADKAR change management as they have common goals. Therefore, there are many technology adoption models that may be applied and tailored to specific projects and to the organizational context and environment. The quantum technologies communications plan benefits from analyzing the adoption determinants and barriers and taking proactive action and messaging.

Each of these quantum technologies adoption determinants can be used in the Quantum Technologies Adoption Readiness Gizmo (Table 7.2) to guide deeper analysis, discussion and actions regarding any barriers and adoption opportunities. Using Gizmos in a workshop setting may enhance team building due to the nature of this cocreation activity; stakeholders discuss, analyze, and progress together.

There are many technology adoption and change management models available to the practitioner. However, there is a sweet spot between model complexity and ease of use. Often when models (and tools, processes, policies, and procedures) are simple like the Deming Cycle for quality management (plan, do, check, and act), adoption is more likely. For that reason, in this book we apply, tailor, and combine the Davis Technology Adoption Model with the ADKar change management approach.

Table 7.2 Quantum technologies adoption readiness Gizmo

Quantum technologies adoption readiness	Rate, discuss, and act	Rating High Low
Perceived usefulness from quantum technologies	What is the perceived usefulness of quantum technologies to the organization, department and people?	5 – 4 – 3 – 2 – 1
Perceived ease of use with quantum technologies	What is the perceived ease of use of quantum technologies to the organization, department and people?	5 – 4 – 3 – 2 – 1
Attitude of end users to adopt quantum technologies	How high is the positive quantum technology adoption attitude of end users?	5 – 4 – 3 – 2 – 1
Social influence of others	How strong is quantum champions' influence?	5 – 4 – 3 – 2 – 1
Anxiety using quantum technologies	How much quantum technology adoption anxiety exists in end users?	5 – 4 – 3 – 2 – 1
Self-efficacy using quantum technologies	What are stakeholders' perceptions of their ability to effectively use quantum technologies?	5 – 4 – 3 – 2 – 1
Upskilling opportunities to adopt quantum technologies	How many quantum technology adoption learning opportunities are planned for end users?	5 – 4 – 3 – 2 – 1

Microlearning

Organizational change management is an established discipline with professional certifications, certifying bodies, a body of knowledge, and advanced degrees from universities. Find out more online:

- Review the ACMP *Standard for Change Management* and identify content that can accelerate the front-end of your quantum technologies journey,
- Find out more about building desire and commitment for change and strategies to manage any resistance to change and change fatigue,
- Identify the top three to five key elements that are common to the change management models.

Change Management Best Practices and Recommendations

The many change management models, including technology adoption models, can be compared and simplified to focus on the most important best practices that may lead to quantum technologies adoption. Apply, tailor, and combine these best practices to swiftly progress through the ADKar stage of the organization's quantum journey:

1. **Clear strategy and vision:** Researchers and their models reflecting successful change emphasize having a clear vision and strategy to guide change management;
2. **Engaged and supportive leadership:** Engaged and supportive leadership is crucial for initiating and sustaining change, especially for a decade of quantum technology projects and post-quantum cryptographic migrations (Figure 1.2);
3. **Sustained communication:** Change requires transparent and ongoing communication and feedback to align stakeholders. Design change management communications to proactively address any resistance to the quantum technology program with additional information guided by the "What's in it for me?" question;
4. **People focus:** Change management success depends on individual and group readiness, involvement, and adoption of change initiatives—in essence, building desire and commitment in stakeholders.

Add these best practices to strengthen quantum technologies change management plans. The researchers widely gave change management recommendations that can also be planned and applied to quantum technologies including:

1. **Build buy-in and participation:** Engage and cocreate with employees at all levels to foster ownership and reduce resistance to change. Add cocreation workshops (e.g., quantum technologies awareness and strategy elaboration) that facilitate communication and team building. Using Gizmos can improve engagement and desire;

2. **Start small with quick wins:** Demonstrating early successes builds momentum and satisfaction, and encourages broader acceptance. For instance, procure technologies for today's use that can also support PQC;

3. **Reinforce and embed change:** Use training and support to sustain and scale the change within the organization's culture. The ITIL Service Management practices can support and reinforce the adoption of quantum technologies (e.g., Incident Management practice to achieve the required service management levels).

Taken together, these insights offer guidance for leaders and quantum champions facing quantum technology adoption barriers. Barriers to technology adoption are not new. They have been studied extensively, giving rise to practical frameworks, best practices, and recommendations. While the determinants of adoption may not precisely predict the trajectory of quantum technologies, they can be simplified to spark discussion and drive action. Engaging teams in conversations about these barriers and underlying factors fosters a shared understanding and the cocreation of effective solutions. If the barriers prove significant, they may delay adoption—potentially prompting a compressed schedule strategy later to catch up. Recognizing and addressing these challenges early is critical to achieving a deliberate, sustainable, and successful quantum transformation.

Microlearning

Due to the popularity of the Davis Technology Adoption Model, there are many resources online.

- Have researchers updated the Davis Technology Adoption Model for quantum technologies, artificial intelligence, or QML?
- What new information can be found about the barriers and enablers of quantum technologies in organizations?
- What best practices and recommendations are available from early AI implementations?

CHAPTER 8

Schedule Compression Basics

> *"Minimizing project duration is probably the most frequently addressed problem in construction project scheduling."*
>
> Tomczak and Jaskowski (2020), 224, 523

Schedule compression or shortening the duration of the project schedule is a common strategy in construction projects. With a long history in practice and research, schedule compression techniques offer quantum project stakeholders best practice insights when prioritizing speedy completion (e.g., time on the Priority Triangle, Figure 3.2). There are at least two reasons for schedule compression: (i) owner convenience to prioritize the delivery of quantum technologies and leverage potential early adopter and disruptor benefits, and (ii) make up for lost time due to falling behind an approved schedule or delaying quantum technology-related projects (e.g., post-quantum cryptographic migrations).

In this chapter, we review schedule compression theory to apply to quantum technology projects. We examine the incredible Wuhan field hospital construction projects that were built in 12 days in response to the escalating healthcare requirements caused by the COVID-19 pandemic in 2020. There are many schedule compression lessons learned that can be summarized as critical success factors applicable to accelerated quantum technology projects.

Schedule Compression: Proceed With Caution

Schedule compression involves advanced techniques often accompanied by greater risk and uncertainty. Therefore, use these scheduling techniques with caution, especially if the fundamentals of project scheduling are weak in the project team.

Indeed, applying schedule compression techniques to quantum technology projects should be considered carefully as new vulnerabilities could be introduced to the organization's digital ecosystem: "It is essential to understand that a hasty migration to post-quantum security systems can introduce new vulnerabilities which could be exploited using conventional hacking methods. These vulnerabilities might arise from oversights, design flaws, or errors in implementation. There could also be issues related to interoperability and backward compatibility, complicating the migration process (Mosca and Piani 2024, 10). Treat the risks related to oversights, design flaws, and implementation errors first by understanding schedule compression theory and then applying the *right* amount of schedule compression. There are two main categories of schedule compression: mathematical and tactical.

Mathematical Schedule Compression

Mathematical project schedule optimization techniques can be used on quantum technology projects. Mathematical techniques like Monte Carlo simulations can help determine the optimal amount of activity overlap to minimize the schedule duration and overall costs (Martins et al. 2023). The mathematical side of schedule compression and optimization has been studied for decades. For example, in the 1960s linear programming was applied to schedules, the Critical Path Method to schedule compression, and integer linear programming to optimize crashing (Ballesteros-Pérez et al. 2019, 230).

A common goal of these techniques is to find combinations of activities to minimize both completion time and costs. Quantum technology projects using compressed schedule techniques are likely to share the same optimization goal. Hence, use mathematical techniques (Table 8.1) in the project planning phase and after a preliminary budget and schedule have been created to find the right schedule for the project. There is a risk that a project schedule can be generated that optimizes the schedule but may not be feasible with the existing teams or the supply chain; therefore, any mathematically optimized project schedule should be reviewed for feasibility by the people scheduled to complete the work. Indeed, a "perfect" mathematically optimized project schedule may not be feasible when reviewed by those responsible for completing the schedule activities.

These, and emerging optimization approaches, are developed and refined in postgraduate, PhD, and other research activities that require advanced mathematics and modeling skills. Ballesteros-Pérez (2019, 233) and his team researched and modeled the cost of crashing an activity which these mathematicians consider *easy* that may be true when you have a PhD grounded in advanced mathematics (Figure 8.1). Incidentally, this is an example of the modeling skill to recruit for should the project require advanced scheduling requirements.

Table 8.1 Mathematical schedule compression models (partial list)

Mathematical Schedule Compression Models (Partial List)	
Heuristics	Linear programming
Genetic algorithms	Fuzzy programming
Mixed integer programming	Non-linear programming
Simulated annealing	Branch and bound algorithms
Dynamic programming	Ant colony optimization
Particle swarm optimization	Tabu metaheuristic search
Integer programming	Constraint programming
Monte Carlo simulation	Combinations of the above techniques

"It may be useful on some occasions to understand the additional cost associated with crashing an activity. The cost increment can *easily* be calculated as detailed below" (Ballesteros-Perez 2019, 233).

$$\Delta C_i = C_{if} - C_{io} = (r_i + n_i + m_i + \frac{1}{n_i} d_i v_i)$$

$$- (r_i + m_i + d_i v_i) = (n_i - 1)m_i + \left(\frac{1 - n_i}{n_i} \right) d_i v_i$$

$$= (n_i - 1)m_i + \left(\frac{1 - n_i}{n_i^{-ai}} \right) d_i v_i = (n_i - 1)m_i + (n_i^{ai} - 1) d_i v_i$$

Figure 8.1 Mathematical example of the cost of crashing

PMOs will increasingly seek project controls professionals with advanced skills in mathematical analysis, modeling, and optimization as project management evolves to use technologies like QML and quantum computing. These new SMEs will perform combinatorial optimization calculations to optimize schedules and budgets during the project plan phase. These specialists, often found in construction firms or universities, may hold certifications like PMI's Scheduling Professional (PMI-SP). Sourcing such rare expertise may require longer lead times and without it, creating and implementing a feasible and optimized compressed schedule is unlikely.

While mathematical schedule optimization techniques are typically applied after project initiation and during the planning phase, schedule compression can also be considered earlier—when quantum strategies are developed in the ADKar phase (Figure 1.1). We recommend *first* considering schedule compression feasibility in the pre-project phase (ADKar) rather than later in the project phase (adkAr).

Microlearning

Mathematical schedule compression techniques are either a mathematical playground for some or a nightmare activity! Find out more about these techniques if you wish to accelerate project schedules:

- What mathematical schedule compression techniques are used in your industry?
- Does your organization's scheduling software support advanced schedule compression techniques like Monte Carlo analysis? Can it use AI to optimize? If so, look for online demos to further explore their capabilities.
- How can activity total and free float be used to increase responsiveness and adaptability and reduce risks?
- Are there data analytics or operations research programs at local universities to find future quantum SMEs to assist with risk management and advanced scheduling techniques?

Tactical Compression Techniques

Besides mathematical schedule compression techniques, there are also tactical ways to finish early. Consider schedule compression first in the strategy phase (pre-project) to determine whether and to what degree schedule compression is required. A key input to compression strategy is first to understand the basics of schedule compression theory, then to determine whether the project teams can implement complex schedule compression techniques. Therefore, understanding schedule compression theory and techniques can improve the probability of developing an appropriate schedule compression strategy aligned with the capabilities of the organization's project teams.

There are multiple ways to compress a schedule; however, substitution, crashing, and fast tracking are the most common techniques used in projects and can be applied to and tailored for quantum technology projects.

Substituting

Finishing sooner by substituting "slow" activities with "speedy" activities is a common schedule compression technique. Some slow (long-duration) activities can be substituted with fast (short) duration activities but are likely more expensive. For instance, the project schedule may be shortened using component prefabrication rather than assembling and configuring components by the project team during the project build phase. Pre-configured technology with secure-by-design components are examples of substitution (e.g., pre-configured by the supplier, rather than secured by the IT team during the project's build phase).

Crashing

Crashing a schedule is adding more resources to the project like people or equipment. Crashing a schedule is appropriate when the project priority is a speedy completion (Figure 3.3, Marketing's priority). The priority shifts to time in the Priority Triangle with the imminent arrival of a cryptographically-relevant quantum computer—Q-Day—and the organization responds by crashing resources to migrate high priority data and systems to PQC.

Crashing has a "sweet spot" and adding too many resources can be counterproductive. For example, there may be a simple initiative to paint a 20-person meeting room with one painter that can be finished in two days. However, using four painters will likely result in finishing sooner (e.g., crashed schedule). While four painters cost more (a common effect of adding more resources), it is likely that four painters will finish *paint the meeting room* activity faster than one painter. However, there is an upper limit to effective crashing; sometimes adding extra workers can delay a project (e.g., adding 40 people to paint the same meeting room will delay the project since there are more people to coordinate and at some point, too many people will start to get in each other's way).[31] Consequentially, for each task, there is a schedule compression "sweet spot" where an ideal number of workers can be used to optimize completion times and costs.

Finding the optimal amount of crashing is extremely challenging as most compressed schedule projects struggle in practice to meet their aggressive targets. For instance, to substantially compress a schedule with crashing (e.g., 10,000 construction workers on the Leishenshan COVID-19 hospital construction site), many diverse resources and workers are often required which is extremely difficult to coordinate. Crashing coordination improves with deliberate and frequent communication, co-location of the project team, and on-site supervision (Lu et al. 2023, 3699). Brooks (1975) pointed out that crashing software development projects is especially difficult since the work requires specialized knowledge (e.g., quantum computing).

---

[31]Frederick Brooks wrote *The Mythical Man-Month* (1975) about software engineering projects and schedule delays. He learned the hard way working on large IBM technology projects that adding more resources often delays the project which is counterintuitive. However, adding more human resources (crashing) results in an increased number of people that are involved in the communication channels with increased communication-related risks. As a result, we have Brooks Law: Adding more people to late projects makes it later. So, shortening IT schedules has been a project manager's goal since the earliest days of information technology projects.

There are many ways to crash a schedule like adding weekend and evening work to catch up (e.g., "overtime crashing"). Adding overtime work on weekends and evenings is not a sustainable practice, especially on long-duration projects. A more sustainable but costly crashing approach is to add and resource additional teams to crash the project schedule. For example, hire extra people (if you can find these specialized resources) so that work can continue during the weekend without regular staff working overtime.

While crashing can reduce the schedule duration, there is an optimal number of resources that can be added to expedite a schedule. Above that sweet spot, work becomes congested, and resources are wasted. Therefore, crashing increases project costs with additional risks of delay due to more resources to coordinate. Effective risk management, again, is a critical success factor for successful schedule compression when using the crashing technique.

Fast Tracking

Fast tracking is an activity overlapping technique to compress a schedule to deliver activities sooner. The purpose of fast tracking is to save time and money by overlapping many or a few activities and/or project phases (Figure 8.2). Overlapping activities in the plan and design phases *may* result in schedule compression and time savings but without adding significant costs like in the schedule crashing technique. For instance, in weeks 3 and 4, there are some planning activities overlapped with design activities. While *Overlapped Activities* (P-027 and D-002) are often displayed as in Figure 8.2, overlapping activities can occur anywhere within the project phase and not necessarily in overlapping phase segments. Here, an early planning activity P-004 may be completed and not impact a late occurring design activity D-0026. However, P-004 may overlap with another planning activity like P-010. Likewise, the planning activity P-027 overlaps with the design activity D-002 but not D-004. However, D-002 overlaps with the design activity D-004. And the design activity D-026 has no overlap.

The complexity of overlapping activities is apparent from even simple examples like that in Figure 8.2. With overlapped activities and phases

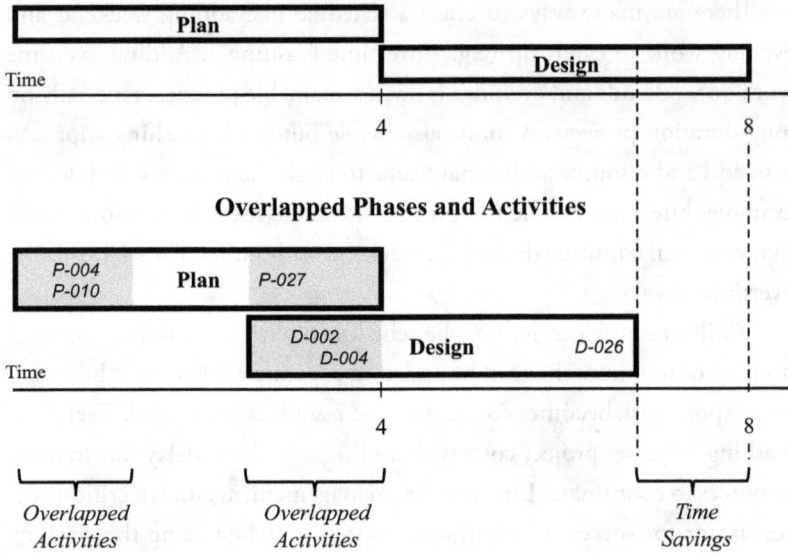

Figure 8.2 Fast tracked activities and project phases

there is more complexity, more risks and uncertainty. Complexity, uncertainty, and risks are compounded as a static schedule becomes fluid to respond to change. And the quantum project environment in which the team follows the schedule may be characterized as VUCA (Volatility, Uncertainty, Complexity, and Ambiguity) that leads to even more risk. These are the types of details that are analyzed, managed, and monitored during schedule creation, implementation through to closure—a full-time job! So, build in sufficient time to continuously analyze overlapped activities and phases for their risks and make the necessary adjustments to achieve project objectives.

Fast Tracking Is Risky

As a public service announcement, most fast track projects fail to achieve their objectives, so proceed with caution when using these techniques! The fast track approach has had very public project failures like the Brandenburg Airport, which was 14 years late; the Delhi Metro Phase III, which was four years late; or Boston's "Big Dig" transportation project, which was nine years late. Fast tracking is risky, which calls for mature project and risk management practices.

Generally, the amount of schedule overlap varies from partial to extensive, where partial activity overlap is less risky than extensive activity overlap (Maraqa et al. 2022, 2). Therefore, more activity overlap results in more schedule risks and uncertainty, especially as the number of critical paths increase. Check that previously noncritical paths have not become critical paths. Identify and track risky overlapped activities in a risk register. For instance, a risk statement can be written: "Due to late changes in Activity P-027, there is a risk that the downstream and concurrent activity D-002 may have design errors, resulting in rework." D-002 may be a costly activity to repeat, and cost overrun risks for this activity may be added to the risk register. Notice that the risk statement included the activity numbers of the work at risk that allows for easier monitoring and follow-up.

The key implication of fast tracking is the expanded degree of concurrency (more overlapping activities) in these time-driven projects resulting in multiple critical paths—more concurrency, more risk, and more uncertainty. Project planners evaluate risks and determine which activities to overlap and the degree of overlap, activity evolution, and sensitivity (Bogus et al. 2011, 950). The amount of appropriate overlap is related to the duration and evolution of an upstream activity development and the downstream activity's sensitivity to change.

Fast tracking can increase the quantity of critical activities and paths and decrease the total float of noncritical activities. Total float is the time an activity can be delayed without affecting the project's completion date. Thus, using total float to compress critical activities makes the project more vulnerable and intolerant of schedule delays (Turkoglu et al. 2023, 627). Caution is advised when using total float to compress the project schedule. It is far better to use free float to compress the schedule. Free float is the time one can delay an activity without impacting the earlier possible start of the successor activity.

For this reason, it is essential to conduct a risk analysis for *most overlapping activities* on the critical path(s) to prevent and mitigate rework. Again, such an analysis takes considerable time that extends the planning period for compressed schedule projects over projects where the priority is not on fast schedule completion. During this diligent analysis of quantum technologies project work, keep in mind that there may be a risk scenario for late adopters that their internal and external teams may lack experience with these technologies (e.g., this is their first time to migrate to PQC) which introduces additional risks.

Risk of Rework

The number one risk in fast tracking is that downstream activities may need to be reworked if upstream activities change; indeed, there may be a risk that a large amount of rework may negate any realized benefits from fast tracking. Add the risk of rework to the risk register as a general place-holder, then identify and manage rework risks associated with specific activities (e.g., "Due to changes in upstream Activity P-027, there is a risk that Activity D-002 may require rework ...", see Figure 8.2). Conse-quently, diligence and analysis are required when considering overlapping to compress the project schedule, since there are increased risks of waste, rework, schedule delays, and cost overruns, all leading to an increased quantity of change requests to process, analyze, approve, and integrate. Optimizing the change management process can be included in the tech-nical maturity projects (Figure 1.2).

Best practices guide schedule compression to be strategic and mea-sured, and an early decision, followed by a lean compressed schedule implementation process that is planned, managed, monitored, and con-trolled. However, loose or informal schedule compression planning and analysis often results in defective schedules due to applying low schedule maturity practices. Hence, a common practice in compression projects is continuous planning and risk management (e.g., better to prevent risks than to resolve issues).

Activity Compression Analysis and Risk Identification

To prevent and mitigate the amount of rework, planners analyze the sched-ule and identify its risks to understand the feasibility and impact of overlap-ping activities. The degree of activity uncertainty and complexity is related to the nature of the activity. Upstream or predecessor activities may evolve quickly or slowly; this activity evolution information is shared with down-stream successor activity participants where these activities vary in sensitivity to changes in upstream activities.[32] For instance, design information may evolve slowly or quickly until it is approved; it starts with a broad range of options and evolves into an approved design. A fast-evolving activity develops its information early in its activity duration versus a slow evolving activity where its information is developed late in its activity life cycle. So, upstream activities evolve on a continuum of slow to fast *evolution*. There is also a continuum of high to low downstream activity *sensitivity* to changes in upstream activities. Sensitivity is how a downstream activity reacts to upstream changes; for example, does rework to a downstream activity require a week of effort or is the rework a minor change that only needs 10 minutes of effort? Also consider the cost of rework and the benefits of getting it right the first time and avoiding rework.

The analysis process is straightforward but cumbersome, requiring diligence: Identify overlapping activities, then analyze the type of upstream activity evolution compared to downstream activity sensitivity to change (and especially in a VUCA project environment). Such analysis is more complex when relationships are one to many (e.g., one upstream activity directly affects multiple downstream activities) and when there are multiple critical paths like in compressed schedules.

Analyze the four types of overlapping activity relationships to develop a feasible compressed schedule:

1. **Slow Evolution Predecessor and High Sensitivity Successor:** This type of relationship is the riskiest to overlap and careful analysis, implementation, monitoring and control are required. Upstream activities (predecessors) evolve slowly like developing the detailed design documents that impact high sensitivity downstream (successor) activities like procurement. Slow evolution/high sensitivity overlapped activities benefit from proactive risk treatment to prevent risks from occurring (e.g., develop the appropriate level of project and service management maturity to specifically manage compressed activities).

---

[32]Quantitative researchers view downstream activities like dependent variables and upstream activities like independent variables. Modeling equations are then developed with dependent and independent variables.

2. **Fast-Evolution Predecessor and Low-Sensitivity Successor:** This type of overlapping relationship carries the least risk and is amenable to overlapping. Upstream activities (predecessors) evolve rapidly, such as opting for Quantum-as-a-Service (QaaS) instead of building an on-premises quantum computer, while having less impact on low-sensitivity downstream (successor) activities. Also, conducting a cryptographic inventory of an organization's digital ecosystem is essential and is unlikely to be significantly affected by changes in upstream activities. In general, low-sensitivity activities require minimal rework when upstream activities are altered.

3. **Fast-Evolution Predecessor and High-Sensitivity Successor:** These activity relationships have moderate risk and benefit from risk management for their successful completion. Some upstream activities (predecessors) may evolve quickly like prioritizing which business units (e.g., manufacturing) will be the first to experiment with and adopt quantum technologies that impact high sensitivity downstream (successor) activities like training for key stakeholders (e.g., process engineers) in the prioritized business units.

4. **Slow-Evolution Predecessor and Low-Sensitivity Successor:** These activity relationships have moderate risk and require routine risk management for their successful completion. These upstream activities (predecessors) evolve slowly like revising the supply chain cryptographic agility policy and procedures that impact low-sensitivity downstream (successor) activities like creating penetration testing checklists for new quantum technologies.

Simply, some downstream activities are more difficult to change, while some upstream activities take longer to develop resulting in higher volatility for some downstream activities. Therefore, evaluate risks for overlapping activities to understand and analyze their evolution and sensitivity rates (Figure 8.3) illustrated in a matrix (inspired by Bogus et al. 2011, 951).

While successfully compressing a schedule throughout the project delivery process is an extraordinarily complex and somewhat rare occurrence, one may be inspired by the expert wood cutter (and American politician, Abraham Lincoln) who wrote: "Give me six hours

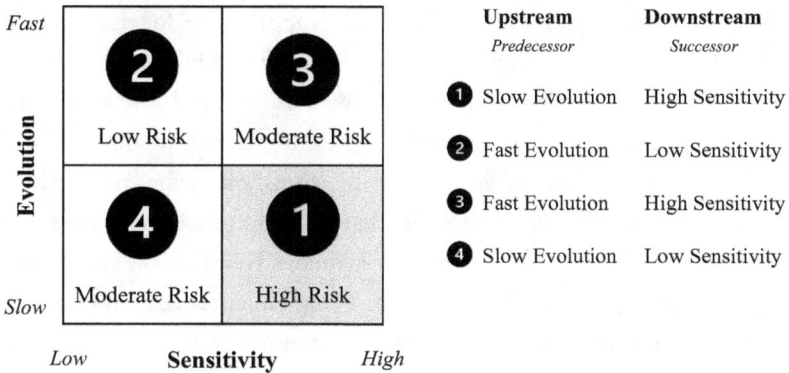

	Upstream	Downstream
	Predecessor	*Successor*
❶	Slow Evolution	High Sensitivity
❷	Fast Evolution	Low Sensitivity
❸	Fast Evolution	High Sensitivity
❹	Slow Evolution	Low Sensitivity

Figure 8.3 Activity evolution and sensitivity risk matrix

to chop down a tree and I will spend the first four sharpening the axe." Therefore, developing a feasible compressed schedule requires continuous planning, activity analysis, and adaptation as the project progresses.

To better understand overlapping activity risks, the project manager can facilitate workshops to identify high-risk activities by reviewing the critical path and analyzing activity relationships as per the activity evolution and sensitivity risk matrix (Figure 8.3). Create and use checklists to guide activity evolution and sensitivity analysis to reduce risks and achieve the intended quality.

Some project managers may wish to avoid or minimize overlapping activities in category 1 (Figure 8.3, slow evolution and high sensitivity overlapping activities). To do so, adjust the schedule to minimize the number of these risky overlapping activities (slow evolution and high sensitivity) to create a less risky schedule. Less risky activities like those in category 2 are more easily overlapped (fast evolution and low sensitivity). Activities that are in category 3 (fast evolution and high sensitivity) and category 4 (slow evolution and low sensitivity) have moderate risks and require regular and frequent risk management (e.g., monitoring to effectively manage activity overlap completion). Finding the optimized mix of overlapping activities that consider sensitivity, and evolution may be like untying the Gordian Knot; instead, perhaps begin with a *moderate* amount of overlap and see if compression is feasible with the project teams and level of technical maturity.

Less overlap (e.g., 20 percent or less[33]) is appropriate for risky activity pairs that are characterized by slow evolution and high sensitivity. For simple activities characterized with slow evolution and low sensitivity, moderate overlap may be possible (e.g., 40 percent to 60 percent). Evaluate the amount of overlap in a workshop using the activity evolution–sensitivity risk matrix (Figure 8.3) and update the risk register. The amount of risk in a compressed schedule is based on the degree and type of activity overlap all other things being equal. This analysis is best completed through teamwork, collaboration, and cocreation which leads to task ownership and effective project teams.

Activity evolution and sensitivity analysis help teams to identify and analyze risks required to optimize compressed project schedules. Analyze the optimized schedule for risks (Figure 9.3 discussed later) then proceed to quality control (find and fix defects). Later, the Defense Contract Management Agency (DCMA) 14-Point Assessment tool is introduced to show the reader the variety of quality control methods available to find and fix schedule defects leading to improved schedules.

Concurrent Engineering

Concurrent engineering is a type of fast tracking where quality is the main priority. The priority in fast track projects is to accelerate the schedule and finish sooner than an uncompressed schedule. While these two techniques overlap activities, in this book, the project priority is on time and to accelerate the front-end of the quantum technologies change management program of projects. For this reason, there is more fast track content rather than concurrent engineering techniques in *Accelerated Quantum*.

---

[33]These estimates (20 percent, 40 percent, and 60 percent) are derived from research about compressed schedule construction projects that had high complexity. Therefore, there are some similarities to quantum technologies schedule compression projects where at the time of publishing this book, there are no extant research regarding compressed schedule quantum technologies projects. Use these construction project estimates as rough order of magnitude estimates for quantum technology compressed schedule projects and adjust them based on your organization's technical maturity stack and the competencies of your teams.

When reviewing compressed schedule projects, there are obvious conclusions. First, the most common schedule compression techniques are fast tracking, crashing, and substitution. Second, these are complex techniques inviting more project risk and uncertainty and often resulting in change requests and schedule delays due to rework. This chain reaction risk can lead to disputes and litigation. Third, these techniques can be extremely successful when technical maturity practices including risk management are sufficient and effectively applied by competent project teams and leadership like in the Wuhan hospital case study described next.

Microlearning

There are many resources online about schedule compression:

- Find out about projects that used fast tracking but did not adequately manage their risks resulting in schedule delays (and cost overruns). Hint: Denver International Airport, Sydney Opera House, and the London Crossrail Project,
- Learn more about using free and total float as a risk treatment tactic,
- Watch the historic and entertaining "Three-Hour House" video of a schedule compression competition in 1983 between two teams to build a three-bedroom house in under three hours. Notice the smiles of the competitors who were driven by desire to meet the very aggressive schedule; however, also notice the loose workplace health and safety practices.
- Learn about construction planners who regularly use schedule compression techniques,
- Discover the differences between concurrent engineering and fast tracking in technology projects; which are used in the space industry?
- Discover how the Lean Six Sigma approach is used to optimize processes like ITIL processes to plan, implement, and optimize quantum technologies.

Wuhan Hospitals Case Study

Fast tracking is one of the most common approaches to schedule compression in the construction industry and there are key lessons learned that may be applied to quantum technology projects. For example, extraordinary stories emerged about extreme schedule compression projects in Wuhan, China, to provide extra hospital beds during the COVID-19 pandemic in 2020. Common to most countries, Wuhan hospitals were overwhelmed with sick people that exceeded the local healthcare system's capacity to provide care. Therefore, projects were initiated to plan, design, build, and commission two specialty COVID-19 field hospitals, Huoshenshan and Leishenshan—with extremely compressed construction schedules: 9 and 12 days (Chen et al. 2021, 3, Figure 8.4)! The planners learned from the Beijing Xiaotangshan Hospital, which was also built following a compressed schedule strategy to open quickly and treat severe acute respiratory syndrome (SARS) patients in 2003. There were lessons learned from the 2003 SARS hospital compressed schedule project that were subsequently applied to the 2020 Wuhan hospital compressed schedule construction projects.

The Wuhan case studies of "ultra-rapid" also known as "flash track" construction projects are studied by researchers and their results are in the best research journals. Since schedule compression has a long history in construction and demonstrated with recent successes with the Wuhan hospital projects, what can we learn from our construction project management cousins and apply to quantum technology projects?

Figure 8.4 Leishenshan hospital construction

Wuhan Schedule Compression Critical Success Factors

The compressed schedule critical success factors must be managed effectively for project success. The Wuhan hospital construction critical success factors can be applied and tailored to quantum technology projects and categorized as people, processes, and technologies.

People: Schedule Compression Critical Success Factors

Ed Deming, the quality management guru wrote that "leadership was only 99% of the problem" and perhaps the converse is also true. It is no surprise that the Wuhan schedule compression projects had leaders and SMEs throughout the project with significant schedule compression competencies. They had schedule compression *knowledge*, *skills*, and *experience* that were *effectively applied* during the project (Figure 5.1). Experience is measured in number of years and the quality of the experience (e.g., the level of project management maturity experience).

Leadership was at the project site rather than at corporate headquarters resulting in speedy decisions due to being closer to the work.[34] For instance, 100 extra electricians were required and with a single telephone call they appeared on the work site soon after. The ability to quickly adapt and to supply 100 highly skilled practitioners was possible with (i) high *trust* that contractual details could be sorted out later, and (ii) high *desire* for the electricians to support the project with their expertise. Another critical success factor is the Chinese project teams took direction in ways that might not work in other cultures (e.g., they did what they were told). Thus, a sophisticated and capable supply chain (people, technology, and supplies) supported the Wuhan hospital projects.

Project leadership used the crashing technique and applied extra resources to the project: 10,000 construction workers were coordinated in 24/7 shifts over 12 days to build the Leishenshan hospital. Leadership created favorable project conditions for teams to give their best for schedule compression success (e.g., effective communications, project and

---

[34]Tom Peters in his bestselling book *In Search of Excellence* found that successful leaders managed by wandering around to be closer to where work occurred rather than siloed in their corporate office.

construction management maturity, servant leadership style, and colloca-
tion). Leadership harnessed a strong desire in their teams to save lives resulting in extraordinary behavior and schedule compression success. Perhaps
extraordinary desire is necessary for extraordinary schedule compression
project success[35]. If the desire for quantum technologies does not exist,
then organizational change management techniques may be used to create
awareness, desire, and knowledge for quantum technologies (e.g., ADKar).

Process: Schedule Compression Critical Success Factors

Lean, mature, and automated processes supported the compressed schedule hospital construction projects. The Wuhan hospitals were built following advanced project and construction management strategies and plans
aligned with process-based best practices. The value proposition in best
practices is on display here where if the user judiciously applies, tailors,
and combines best practices to the project context, then risks are reduced
and the required level of quality is likely to be achieved. Thus, the role of
sufficiently mature processes in successful projects cannot be overstated.
The quality adage relies upon sufficient process maturity: "good process,
good result." Indeed, following simple processes and using simple tools to
assemble furniture has been a critical success factor for IKEA.

Maturity models guide progressive improvement in processes and
tools. The Wuhan hospital projects began with high levels of process maturity (e.g., project and construction management). Project and construction management maturity allowed the teams to succeed with complex
and risky schedule compression methods.

High project management maturity ("optimized" level) was evident
in many areas. For instance, the project priority was on time and clearly
understood by project teams as they acted as a unit to successfully overlap
design and build activities. Leadership used multiple schedule compression techniques (e.g., crashing, fast tracking, and substituting). Quality

---

[35]The extraordinary desire to contribute to project success was also seen in the
successful rescue of the Thai Wild Boars football team, who were trapped in the
Tham Luang Nang Non cave in July 2018 due to heavy rain and flooding. Here,
adaptive project management (e.g., agile principles and values) was a critical success factor.

was designed-in through standards and regulatory frameworks. Risks were reduced with effective and timely communications and information sharing where the frequency of interactions increased to manage change. For instance, the Leishenshan Hospital construction area was increased two times in six days; the initial plan was for a 50,000 m² hospital that was increased to 70,000 m², and then to 80,000 m². For each change, the project team updated the project plans on-site with collocated teams in real time. The project change management process was lean and effective.

Thus, to improve the probability of successful compressed schedule quantum technology projects, optimize relevant end-to-end processes through to the safe, secure, and environmentally friendly disposition of legacy technologies that complies with the United Nations Sustainable Development Goals (SDG 12, Target 5). The degree of construction and project management maturity (e.g., lean, integrated, and automated processes, tools, and techniques) was sufficient for the amount of schedule compression applied. Hence, quantum technology projects can benefit from the right amount of technical maturity (Table 3.2) delivered through a program of quantum technology projects (Figure 1.2).

Technology: Schedule Compression Critical Success Factors

Another critical success factor for compressed schedule projects is the effective use of technologies and automation. Specifically, automation and building information modeling (BIM) systems, technology substitution, and reverse design methods and processes were cited as critical success factors for schedule compression. In construction, BIM also streamlines the integration of design, budgets, and schedules, making it easier to manage in real time changes at any stage of the project.

Advanced BIM technologies, especially for the design activities, improved process management, real-time collaboration, product quality, and communications, and reduced rework. These technologies aligned design, procure, and build/configure activities resulting in fewer bottlenecks. The right information was available at the right time (e.g., the "source of truth" was accessible). The effective use of these technologies leveraged lean and automated processes that contributed to schedule compression success. For this reason, use integrated project management software that has capabilities to manage activity overlap for schedule compression projects.

BIM and other design simulation technologies aid workers to understand in real time the fluid design and make better build decisions. These technologies also included role responsibility information, so workers knew what they needed to do and who was responsible. These technologies helped to compress the schedule since they reduced the time to validate and approve the design and later approve changes to the design. While digital technologies like BIM systems were used, the team also applied nondigital techniques like optimally situated site offices to increase productivity (e.g., less distance to walk to discuss a problem with a site supervisor).

Substitution techniques also shortened the construction phase on the Wuhan hospital projects. For example, they used the reverse design technique where the design was influenced by what was available in the supply chain inventory rather than creating a design then sourcing the required components that may be out of stock. With the reverse design approach, available inventory and construction specifications drove the design specification thereby avoiding traditional supply chain issues like delays due to out of stock items. The extensive use of prefabrication rather than on-site building and testing was also fundamental to the schedule compression strategy. Here, the Leishenshan hospital was built with over 3,000 prefabricated hospital rooms of two standard sizes to reduce risks and improve quality by *getting it right the first time.*

Workers on the Wuhan hospital projects cite substitution and reverse design as the most innovative elements of the schedule compression strategy (Lu et al. 2023, 3707). AI and automation are digital substitutions for human work that also can be used in projects (e.g., testing). Effective substitution contributed to schedule compression success for the Wuhan hospital construction projects. These digital substitution tools can be tailored, combined, and applied to the decade of project work to plan, implement, and optimize quantum technologies like post-quantum cryptographic migrations. Look for technologies with effective AI and automation capabilities.

The Wuhan hospital projects were successful schedule compression projects for many reasons that have been categorized into people, processes, and technologies. Many of these critical success factors can be applied to quantum technology projects to get an accelerated start and to keep momentum progressing. However, schedule compression techniques are advanced, risky and with a higher probability of failure than noncompressed schedule projects. What worked in Wuhan, China, might not achieve the same results in Regina, Canada, due to a different project context. Indeed, they can be counterproductive where schedule compression fails, leading to schedule delays and cost overruns. So, onboard competent SMEs with successful compressed schedule experience. It is prudent to conduct a gap analysis of schedule compression competencies to determine the recruiting requirements. Project schedule compression success begins with a feasible schedule compression strategy and plan.

To sum up this chapter, use schedule compression strategically— while it can accelerate project timelines, it also introduces complexity and risk. This chapter showed that schedule compression involves two main approaches: mathematical and tactical. With a draft schedule and budget, apply mathematical algorithms to compress and optimize the timeline. In parallel, plan for tactical techniques such as *crashing* and *fast tracking*— people-oriented strategies that adjust how and when work gets done.

Focus your tactical efforts early using tools like the ADKar model to align teams and build momentum. Later, as more project data becomes available (e.g., draft budget), use mathematical compression methods to refine the schedule if necessary. However, make informed decisions from the outset; be careful not to rush into schedule compression without a solid understanding of its methods, best practices, critical success factors, and potential risks. Doing so increases the likelihood of project failure. Instead, take a disciplined, knowledge-driven approach to schedule acceleration that balances speed with stability.

Microlearning

Let's switch it up and use old school techniques to extend your learning. With a pen and paper, draw the Priority Triangle (Figure 3.3) for the Leishenshan Hospital. What are the two top priorities?[36] Think "faster, better, or cheaper; choose two." Compare their project priority to your own quantum technology project priority.

---

[36] Hint, the same as Marketing's priority in Figure 3.3.

CHAPTER 9

Managing the Quantum Compressed Schedule

> *DANGER: Read Instructions Before Using*
> *A common advisory attached to potentially dangerous goods that is often ignored*

Like any technique or machine (e.g., a microwave oven) that has some risk, there are warning labels that advise reading a product manual before use to avoid damage or injury. This chapter serves the purpose to inform and warn about the risks related to using compressed schedule techniques and how to manage their risks to improve the probability of creating a feasible schedule. We wish to share some techniques required to manage a compressed schedule. With this knowledge in the pre-project phase, the reader will better determine whether and to what degree of schedule compression fits the organization's program of quantum technology projects (Figure 1.2).

Successful schedule compression projects begin before project initiation (adkAr) and in the strategy phase (ADKar). Here, leadership first considers whether their project teams and the organization have sufficient competencies and whether the organization has sufficient technical maturity (capability) to successfully compress quantum technology project schedules. Since schedule compression is risky and difficult to execute, accelerating a schedule requires its own strategy. Like the organization's strategies (business, IT, and cybersecurity), developing, planning, and executing the schedule compression strategy is also iterative (Figure 3.6).

When developing a schedule compression strategy, apply and tailor the ITIL Strategy Management practice for quantum technologies projects. Begin with a gap analysis:

1. *Evaluate* the organization's current schedule compression capabilities (e.g., people—internal and external; processes; and technologies) to complete the compressed work according to the schedule, make decisions, and manage the increased number and severity of project risks due to schedule compression. Simply, *can we do it? Do we have sufficient technical maturity to deliver to a compressed schedule? And for how long? Is the pace sustainable? Are there project fatigue risks?*

2. *Define* the compression goals and identify the types of schedule compression methods (e.g., fast tracking and crashing) the organization intends to use in their quantum technology project and,

3. *Implement* the schedule compression strategy and compress the quantum project schedule (adkAr).

The early completion of this analysis (e.g., pre-project) improves the probability the organization can successfully execute a compressed schedule project involving quantum technologies.

1. Evaluate Schedule Compression Capabilities

Conduct a gap analysis to evaluate schedule compression capabilities: What are the organization's *current* schedule compression capabilities and what is the organization's *target* state for schedule compression regarding technical maturity, project type, and team competencies (Figure 9.1)?

Evaluating the feasibility of schedule compression capabilities is complex but can be manageable when using Gizmos in a workshop setting.

Technical Maturity Evaluation

When evaluating schedule compression feasibility, consider the organization's technical maturity (Table 3.2) for at least project, service, and change management maturity. Add cybersecurity management maturity evaluations for cybersecurity projects (e.g., cryptographic agility and post-quantum cryptographic migrations). Applying complex schedule compression techniques in a low technical maturity environment increases risks and uncertainty. Factor in that many quantum technology

Technical Maturity	• Project management
Technical Maturity Capability Gizmo	• Change management
Table 3.2	• Service management
	• Cybersecurity management

Project Type	• Criticality
Project Type Gizmo	• Complexity
Table 9.1	• Priority
	• Urgency

Team Competencies	• Compression
Team Competencies Gizmo	• Technical maturity
Table 9.2	• Project type—attributes

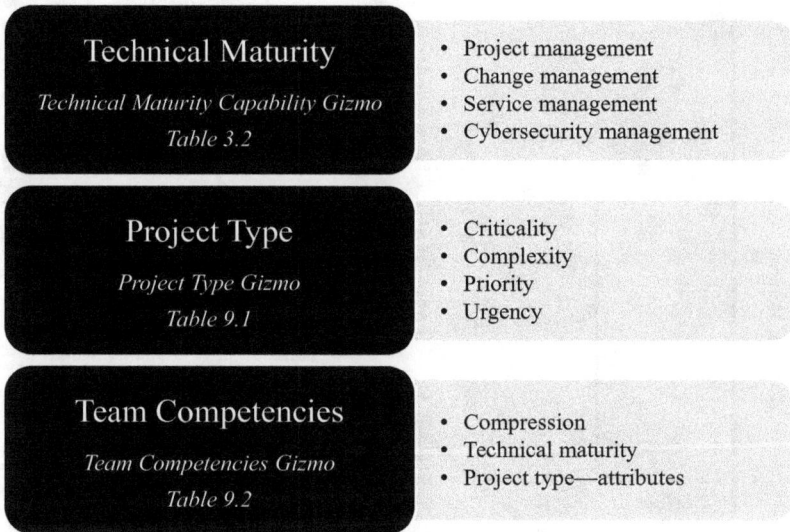

Figure 9.1 Schedule compression feasibility evaluation

projects are inherently complex and delicate even without schedule compression! However, competent people and effective processes and technologies (e.g., sufficient technical maturity) improve the probability of project success with a compressed project schedule.

Schedule compression planners can evaluate their current technical maturity and if there is a gap, then technical maturity projects can be initiated to support the many and sustained quantum technology projects to follow (Figure 9.2).

The slope of the quantum computing line in Figure 9.2 is arbitrary; instead, the main point is to conduct a gap analysis for the organization's technical maturity to prevent unrealistic strategies and expectations for the quantum program of projects (e.g., too much schedule compression beyond the project team's competencies). In Figure 9.2, the organization currently has low or insufficient technical maturity to plan, implement, and optimize quantum technologies. There is a significant gap to reach their target technical maturity. Should the organization implement quantum technologies according to a compressed schedule with their low technical maturity, there is a low probability to successfully implement these complex technologies and may lead to chain reaction risks (Figure 9.3). Chain reaction risks have knock-on effects that may result in multiple

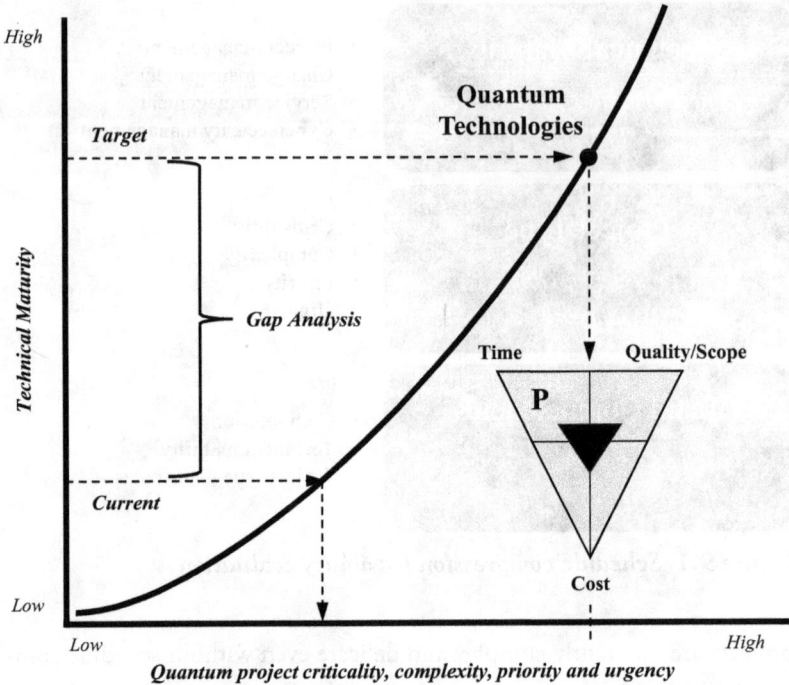

Figure 9.2 Technical maturity and the quantum project attributes

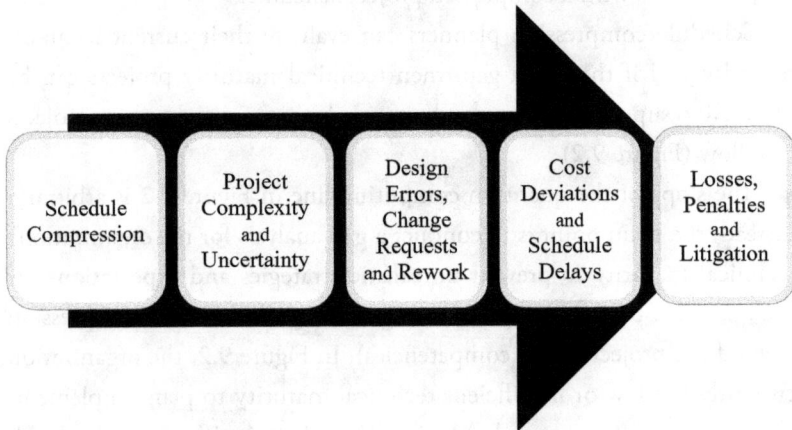

Figure 9.3 Schedule compression chain reaction risks

risks that increase compression schedule complexity and uncertainty. Document any chain reaction risks in the risk register identified during the quantum schedule compression capabilities analysis.

Hence, an early series of projects (Figure 1.2) is to achieve sufficient technical maturity with lean processes and support like procedures and templates to complete the work. Finally, evaluate the type of project being considered to better understand feasibility.

Project Type Evaluation

To better understand the type of project under consideration, evaluate the project's attributes including criticality, complexity, priority, and urgency. Stakeholders can systematically evaluate and discuss each attribute to reach a shared understanding of the type of project being initiated. Use the Project Type Gizmo (Table 9.1) to rate and then discuss the attribute ratings for the quantum project. This Gizmo fosters discussion and engagement, especially when evaluators assign varying ratings to the project's type.

By understanding the attributes of a project, stakeholders can act and make better decisions. Once quantum teams understand the project type, they can evaluate the technical maturity of the organization to plan, implement, and manage these emerging technologies.

Competency Evaluation

Can we do it? is the question behind evaluating the competencies of team members to deliver successful projects according to a compressed schedule (Table 9.2). We distinguish between capabilities and competencies:

Table 9.1 Project type Gizmo

Project attributes	Rate, discuss, and act	Rating	
		High	Low
Criticality	How important is the quantum technology project to achieving the organization's goals and objectives?	5 – 4 – 3 – 2 – 1	
Complexity	What is the perceived complexity of the quantum technologies project?	5 – 4 – 3 – 2 – 1	
Priority	How fast should the quantum technology projects be implemented?	5 – 4 – 3 – 2 – 1	
Urgency	How important is it to quickly complete the quantum project?	5 – 4 – 3 – 2 – 1	

Table 9.2 Team competencies Gizmo

Competencies	Rate, discuss, and act	Rating High Low
Schedule Compression	What are the competencies of the internal and external teams to successfully deliver technology projects according to a compressed schedule?	5 – 4 – 3 – 2 – 1
Technical Maturity	What are the competencies of the teams regarding technical maturity: project, service, change, and cybersecurity management maturity?	5 – 4 – 3 – 2 – 1
Project Attributes	What is the competence of teams in projects that have attributes of high criticality, complexity, priority, and urgency?	5 – 4 – 3 – 2 – 1

capabilities refer to broader, organization-level functions, while competencies relate to individuals' applied knowledge, skills, and experience (Figure 5.1).

Evaluate the competencies of people to plan, manage, and deliver compressed schedule projects. Consider the team's compressed schedule competencies and their technical maturity experience. Experience has both a quantitative and qualitative dimension. The number of years in compressed schedule projects is the quantitative dimension. However, what is the maturity level of those experiences? Were they at the bottom or *ad hoc* level of project management maturity, or at the higher, *optimized* level of maturity for their compressed schedule projects? Experience at higher levels of technical maturity (Table 3.2) improves the probability teams can be effective with a compressed schedule project.

Conclude the evaluation by bringing together the three Gizmo evaluations (Figure 9.1) to better understand your organization's schedule compression capabilities that is also the organization's *current state*. As a word of caution, some self-reported audits can be overly optimistic as opposed to the results from an independent auditor.

2. Define the Schedule Compression Strategy

Use the outputs from the evaluation phase of the gap analysis to define the schedule compression strategy (technical maturity, project type, and team competency analysis are key inputs used to define and develop the compression strategy [Figure 9.4]). The schedule compression strategy is used later to develop and implement the compressed schedule.

Given the difficulty of scheduling complex projects, it is common that compressed schedules are oversimplified and optimistic resulting in unrealistic deadlines, delays, penalties, and disappointed stakeholders. These project shortcomings are the opposite of the intended goals of compressed schedule projects in the first place (Tomczak and Jaskowski 2020, 224523). Therefore, allow time to plan and develop a compressed schedule strategy for complex quantum technology projects. When compressed schedule capability and competency gaps are identified, update the risk register. When significant gaps are identified (severe risks) they may trigger a compression strategy reevaluation.

Schedule compression is first planned at the strategic (ADKar) and then tactical (adkAr) levels. For instance, a strategic decision may be to formally align stakeholders to engage in schedule compression activities and to anticipate its implications with a risk management plan while in the pre-project phase. Before developing a schedule, there are multiple types of schedule compression tactics that make up the strategy and can be considered by planners (Tomczak and Jaskowski 2020, 224523–525):

1. **Assembly line:** Schedule work so that there is a continuous flow and steady rhythm of production (e.g., use agile sprints for post-quantum cryptographic migrations). This type of work

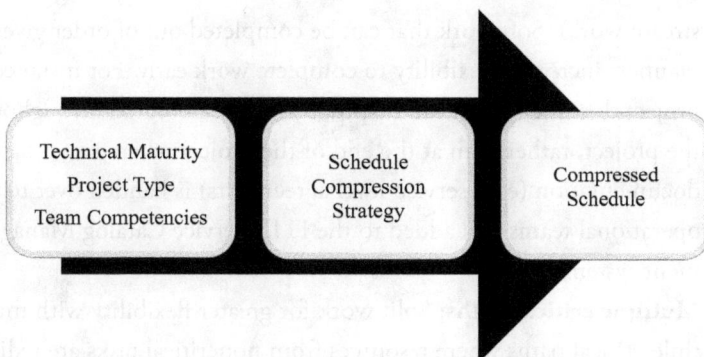

Figure 9.4 Schedule compression strategy flow

requires similar resource requirements (e.g., migrate and validate) and can be delegated as a work package. Also use the assembly line approach to deliver quantum awareness workshops throughout the organization. A key benefit from a design that fosters low-risk repetition of post-quantum cryptographic migrations is that migrations can be assigned to junior cybersecurity SMEs.

2. **Targeted compression:** Apply extra resources or change the mode of execution to quickly complete critical work (e.g., update the organization's "crown jewels" with PQC). Work is typically broken down into smaller work packages and these are analyzed to identify which can be accelerated while minimizing risks and perhaps costs. Adding evening shifts changes the mode of work and can accelerate the project schedule when care and consideration are given to other factors like workplace health and safety risks. Some use prefabrication in the construction industry that reduces project work and can shorten the schedule. Prefabrication is an example of changing the mode of work (e.g., substitution) that has unprecedented effects to compress schedules since there is less work to complete *during* the project because components were prefabricated by a vendor prior to the project. Quantum planners are encouraged to do the same when unprecedented schedule compression is called for in quantum technology projects (e.g., begin by procuring the QaaS rather than building an on-premises quantum computer).

3. **Flexible predecessor:** Arrange work to increase flexibility with "soft" predecessors (e.g., upstream activities) that are less rigid and can begin work early to avoid successor activities delays (e.g., downstream work). Soft work that can be completed out of order gives planners increased flexibility to complete work early. For instance, project documentation can be progressively elaborated throughout the project, rather than at the end of the project where key project documentation (e.g., service-level agreements) is handed over to operational teams and added to the ITIL Service Catalog Management system.

4. **Multiple critical paths:** Split work for greater flexibility with multiple critical paths where resources from noncritical tasks are redirected toward critical tasks with the goal to compress the schedule.

A tactical consideration is to determine the number of critical paths appropriate for the project and team (e.g., dependent upon the technical maturity of the organization and the competence of the quantum teams).

5. **Design for manufacture and assembly:** The design is guided by how fast it can be implemented while meeting appropriate quality standards and regulatory requirements (Tan et al. 2021). For example, design and procure what the vendor has in stock and can be immediately shipped to the project.

6. **Other:** Combine these techniques (e.g., assembly line and targeted compression) to compress schedules.

An early strategy decision is to determine the degree of schedule compression required, if any, after completing the Mosca Theorem risk assessment (Figure 3.2). The organization's capability to implement compressed schedule projects is dependent upon the level of technical maturity including change, project and service management; and cybersecurity maturity for compressed schedule cybersecurity projects. Zero schedule compression leaves untapped opportunities to complete work early, while too much schedule compression leads to increased complexity, risks, and waste. Determining the trade-offs with project sponsors and other stakeholders like SMEs will be unique for each organization and project.

There are many schedule compression considerations including the degree the project environment and operational constraints are conducive to compression, resource competency and availability to adequately support the critical path(s), work logistics, complexity and criticality, contractor's and subcontractors' relationship to successfully accelerate work, the best order of activities to compress, effective risk management to manage additional risks associated with schedule compression, and so forth. These considerations may reveal additional risks to add to the risk register.

How much can a schedule be reduced with schedule compression techniques? Ballesteros-Pérez (2019, 239) researched fast tracking in construction projects and found that it is unlikely to achieve more than 25 percent of the original schedule. Schedule overlap beyond a certain point delivers diminishing returns (Salhab et al. 2024). So, proceed with caution when applying schedule compression to quantum technology projects and perhaps begin with no more than 85 percent compression target (e.g., reduce the original schedule duration by 15%) and revise as necessary.

In the pre-project phase (ADKar) the business, technology, and cybersecurity strategies are *defined* according to the ITIL framework or similarly *developed* according to MBA curricula. Schedule compression is an early consideration should there be a significant gap between the current and target states regarding innovating with quantum technologies and migrating to PQC. Once the quantum technology project is endorsed, approved, and initiated, if a compressed schedule strategy is required, then it is progressively elaborated and implemented throughout the project (adkAr).

3. Implement the Schedule Compression Strategy

Implement the compressed schedule strategy after the definition and evaluation phases of the gap analysis. Document the schedule compression strategy in the project plan. Go through the endorsement process whereby the SMEs who will direct and complete the work endorse that the strategy is fit for purpose and feasible. With their endorsement and incorporated feedback, submit the schedule compression strategy for leadership and project sponsor approval. Accompany the strategy with the risk management plan since a compressed schedule is risky. It is OK to be open and honest with leadership about the project risks and the possibility of failure with a compressed schedule; however, engaged leadership support can greatly reduce risks. For this reason, support the compressed schedule strategy with sufficient technical maturity including a robust risk management plan.

Schedule Compression Risks

While schedule compression promises speedier project completion, these are advanced techniques that have greater inherent risks and uncertainty. Therefore, as more schedule compression is applied, the probability of success decreases if the team and organization have insufficient levels of technical maturity (Figure 9.5). Indeed, applying advanced schedule compression techniques to implement complex technologies like post-quantum cryptographic migrations compounds project risks.

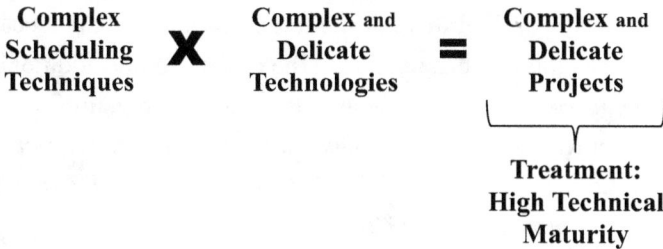

Complex Scheduling Techniques **X** **Complex and Delicate Technologies** **=** **Complex and Delicate Projects**

Treatment: High Technical Maturity

Figure 9.5 Compound and severe risks and treatment

However, reduce the quantity and severity of chain reaction risks with sufficient technical maturity (including robust risk management) which needs to be higher than in regular projects. Begin analyzing schedule compression risks and issues with generally accepted risk management processes (Figure 9.6) and tools like those found in standards (e.g., risk management in the PMBOK Guide or ISO 31001 Risk Management).

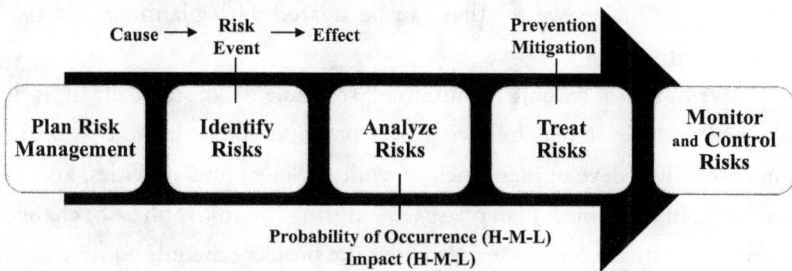

Cause → Risk Event → Effect   Prevention Mitigation

Plan Risk Management **Identify Risks** **Analyze Risks** **Treat Risks** **Monitor and Control Risks**

Probability of Occurrence (H-M-L)
Impact (H-M-L)

Figure 9.6 Generally accepted risk management process

Risk management is a critical success factor for compressed schedule projects; insufficient levels of risk management maturity will likely result in project failure (Rasul et al. 2021, 1107). As project criticality, complexity, priority, and urgency increase (project type) as in many quantum technology projects, so does the necessity for formal risk management. Tune risk management processes and tools during the project management process optimization project (Figure 1.2).

Schedule compression projects benefit from a culture of proactive risk management supported with best practices like weekly project risk status meetings, risk management sections in status reports, and regular risk register use. The standard risk management process (Figure 9.6) underlies the project team's culture. For the rest of the chapter, the focus is on managing schedule compression risks. The reader can find additional risk management resources online about best practices. Program and project risk management are detailed in *Quantum Cybersecurity Program Management* (Skulmoski and Memari 2025a) and in *Shields Up: Cybersecurity Project Management* (Skulmoski 2022).

Plan for Schedule Compression Risks

Begin schedule compression risk management with planning. The purpose of risk management planning is to develop an approach to managing schedule compression risks for quantum technology projects. Simply, risk management planning outlines how the schedule compression strategy (e.g., *targeted compression and crashing*) will be implemented including the processes and tools used to manage risks and, in this case, managing schedule compression risks. We are reminded of the adage "haste makes waste" that can be treated with planning and risk management.

Developing a feasible compressed schedule is more likely if it is planned and developed following best practices like using the WBS to guide schedule development, define work packages and activities, and so on. Thus, in the project plan phase (e.g., during the adkAr phase of change management), the project team follows the project schedule compression strategy to generate a schedule and create a risk management plan.

The technical capabilities (e.g., project, service, and change management maturity) are leveraged throughout the schedule planning process like using planning templates and checklists. The risk management plan for managing compressed schedule risks will include at least the following details: (i) compressed schedule strategy and risk management plan, (ii) risk management process to manage compressed schedule risks and change requests, and (iii) tools like a risk register and integrated technologies to manage the schedule, budget, and compressed schedule risks.

After risk management planning it's time to begin identifying scheduled compression risks and issues.

Identify Schedule Compression Risks

The purpose of risk identification is to find risks sooner than later so that there is more time to treat the risk (e.g., prevent the risk from occurring) and not deviate from the approved project plan should the risk become an issue. There are many ways to identify schedule compression risks including general and focused approaches. For example, simply asking, "What are the risks in this project?" is an example of general risk identification and gets people talking and engaged in the workshop. Focused risk identification targets elements of the project to find risks. For example, a focused risk identification may include the following questions:

- What are the compressed schedule risks in the design phase? Build phase? Test phase? Transition to production phase?
- What are the risks related to the critical path activities? The vendor's critical path activities? The client/owner/sponsor's critical path activities?
- What are the risks related to multiple critical paths?
- What are the risks related to overlapping design, procure, and build activities?
- What are the most sensitive downstream activities on the critical path?
- What are the most expensive activities on the critical path?
- What are the slowest design activities to evolve?
- Which activities are most risky when overlapped?
- What are the risks related to communications and overlapped activities?
- What are the handover risks related to overlapped activities?
- What if the planned action does not work? What should we do? and so forth.

Use these focused risk identification prompts in a workshop setting to identify compressed schedule risks.

Subsystem Integration Risks

A typical schedule compression risk is subsystem integration difficulties. System and subsystem integration is the process of combining different work packages (subsystems like hardware and software) into a cohesive system that works according to the approved design (e.g., quantum technologies that provide the intended value as outlined in the business case). Given the increased number of risks and issues related to compression projects in general and specifically with quantum technology projects due to their complexity (e.g., cryptographic discovery inventory), it is best practice to use a tool like a risk register to document and manage risks (Table 9.3). Risk identification can be structured into a risk statement (cause–risk event–effect) for improved readability and shared understanding.

Generally fast track scheduling projects often face system and subsystem integration risks where there may be design misfits identified during testing resulting in design, build, and test phases rework. Integrated teams are best situated to plan, manage, and support these activities in the design, procure, and build phases and manage subsystem integration risks.

An integrated team is multidisciplinary (e.g., project sponsor, quantum algorithm developer, electrical engineer, business analyst, project manager, and cybersecurity architect) and collaborates throughout the project life cycle. Team members may have multiple roles like being both a project manager and quantum champion. This

Table 9.3 Risk register syntax for a procurement risk

Risk statement			
Cause	Risk event	Effect	Comment
Due to the delayed delivery of quantum sensors (2–3 months),	There is a risk that sensor testing with the new software may be delayed,	Resulting in repeating some testing when the sensors arrive later in the project.	Some workflows with sensors might be able to be tested with synthetic data mitigating the delay.

"act as a unit" trait[37] promotes improved communication and productivity since the right people are available to do the work, make decisions, and give approval.

Chain Reaction Risks

Risk identification is more thorough when chain reaction risks are deliberately identified. For instance, schedule compression techniques are inherently complex with higher uncertainty which may lead to design errors, change requests, and rework. These risks may then trigger cost deviations and schedule delays if not sufficiently treated. These risks may lead to losses and penalties for project stakeholders. The thing about many chain reaction risks in schedule compression projects is the risk severity (probability and impact) can be quickly amplified due to the nature of their interconnectedness. Ask: If this risk becomes an issue, what other risks and issues will arise (e.g., a chain reaction)? Again, provide adequate time at the front-end and throughout the project for risk management, since it is a critical success factor in projects and especially in compressed schedule projects with complex deliverables.

Waste Risks

Waste risks (e.g., design errors and rework) are the most common risks due to overlapping design and build activities that may result in a chain reaction of schedule delays and likely cost overruns. Therefore, purposely look for design error risks that may result in waste and rework, especially for high-cost work packages. Another form of waste is waiting time that is managed with schedule optimization techniques. Waiting time is when downstream work is behind its approved start date due to upstream work finishing after the target date in the approved schedule. Identify upstream activities that may result in severe downstream activity waiting risks and

---

[37]The successful Cleveland Clinic healthcare system has "act as a unit" as its motto that brings caregivers together to deliver world-class care and innovative research and development.

increased costs. Consider adding rework and waste risks to the quantum project risk register, as they are common to schedule compression projects. Once risks are identified, the project team analyzes the risks.

Analyze Schedule Compression Risks

Once risks are identified (Figure 9.6), they are analyzed to determine their risk severity; project teams prioritize high severity risks (high probability and high impact) for treatment. There are many ways to analyze risks including quantitative and qualitative risk assessments. Quantitative risk analysis requires large volumes of data, significant time, and specialized competencies and software; however, there is seldom time to perform quantitative analyses for compressed schedule projects. A quantitative assessment will yield results like there is an 82.3 percent probability the delivery may be late or the impact on the project will be a 9-day delay. Instead, start with a qualitative risk analysis because it is simple and quick; add quantitative analyses if required. Qualitative risk assessments follow a three-step process:

1. **Determine the probability:** evaluate the probability or likelihood the risk may occur. Use high, medium, or low probability of occurrence in the analysis.
2. **Determine the impact:** evaluate the impact on the project if the risk occurs. Use high, medium, or low to describe the degree of impact.
3. **Determine the risk severity:** the probability of occurrence multiplied by the impact if the risk occurs. The qualitative measures are assigned quantitative values in the risk register: High = 3, Medium = 2, and Low = 1. Therefore, a high probability risk with medium impact would be $3 \times 2 = 6/9$ severity. This simple calculation is useful in risk registers to sort risks by severity and priority for treatment, monitoring, and control.

Use this qualitative risk assessment approach to analyze overlapped activity relationships (e.g., evolution rate and sensitivity). Like risk identification, the qualitative risk assessment details are logged in the risk (and issue) register. Qualitative assessments are appropriate for most technology project risks and in the rare time more risk information is required, then quantitative techniques can be used like Monte Carlo simulation. After developing the draft budget and schedule, planners can use mathematical approaches (e.g., activity evolution and-sensitivity analysis, Figure 8.3) to find the "best" schedule for the project. However, caution is advised; increased overlap may result in an unworkable schedule. So, analyze not only the critical path for risks but also other paths through the schedule that may become critical.

Once the compressed project schedule has been optimized for the required risk profile and before schedule approval, planners can use quality control approaches to find any defects in the schedule (Winter 2011, 23), for example:

1. **Logic:** identify any missing predecessors and successors,
2. **Negative lags:** identify any relationships with negative lag durations,
3. **Long lags:** identify any long lag durations,
4. **Hard constraints:** identify any activities that cannot be moved.

Compressed schedule defects can cause delays and/or rework; so, the project benefits from a systematic quality control review prior to baselining the schedule. No doubt by the time you are reading this book, there are likely dozens of AI tools to aid project scheduling including compressed schedule simulation, analysis, and optimization.

To plan, develop, evaluate, and implement the schedule, follow a process (Figure 9.7) supported with checklists and other tools. Make a preliminary decision in the pre-project and quantum strategy phase to use schedule compression tactics after careful analysis; determine if schedule compression is appropriate given the teams' competence and organizational capabilities. Once the project is initiated and moves into the planning phase, the project manager and team progressively elaborate the schedule compression strategy and tactics for the quantum technology project. The team iteratively develops a compressed schedule and may apply mathematical techniques to optimize the schedule.

Project Boundaries - adkAr

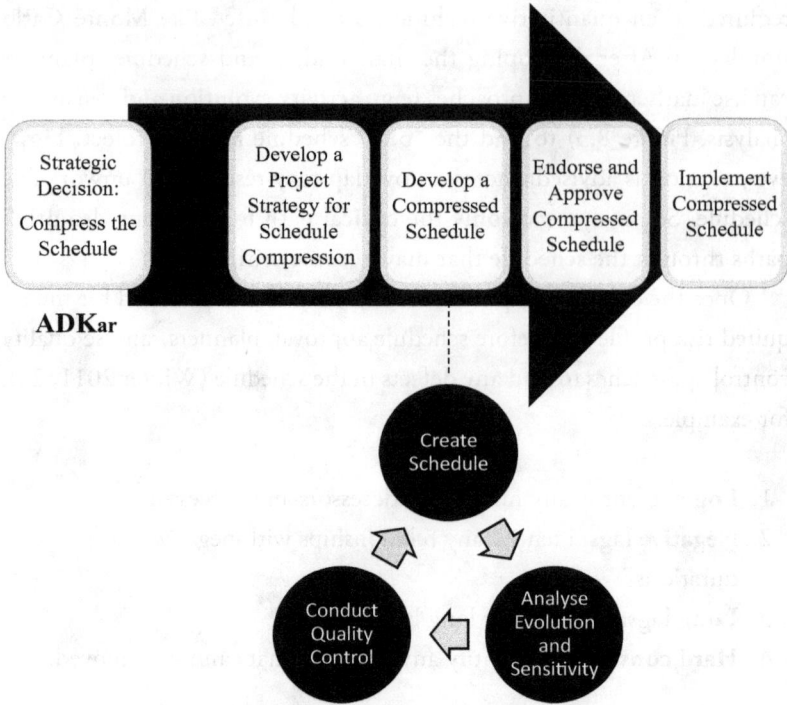

Strategic Decision: Compress the Schedule

Develop a Project Strategy for Schedule Compression

Develop a Compressed Schedule

Endorse and Approve Compressed Schedule

Implement Compressed Schedule

ADKar

Create Schedule

Conduct Quality Control

Analyse Evolution and Sensitivity

Figure 9.7 Compressed schedule development process

For a more thorough analysis of the compressed schedule, analyze the schedule logic using checklists like the Defense Contract Management Agency Schedule Analyzer.[38] Also analyze for feasibility upstream activity evolution and its effect on downstream activity sensitivity and risk. The team of SMEs will endorse the schedule when they have enough confidence in it; there is a sweet spot in schedules where not too much, nor too little detail is the goal. After endorsement, provide the compressed schedule (and project plan) to leadership including the project sponsorship for approval to proceed to implement the schedule.

Consequently, the decision to use advanced schedule compression techniques in quantum technology projects ideally is made after careful

---

[38]See Appendix for the comprehensive Defense Contract Management Agency Schedule Analyzer approach to find schedule defects.

consideration in the strategy development phase (ADKar) which can reduce risks for subsequent project teams. Allow time for this compressed schedule development process to improve the probability of a feasible schedule.

An "ideal" compressed schedule allows for adaptability (e.g., resilience to uncertainty and change). Adaptability is fostered with modularization of technology components for ease of installation and standardization to improve the probability of fit for purpose (e.g., the right quality). These elements are designed into the strategy and schedule. Once schedule compression risks have been identified and analyzed, the next step in the risk management process is to treat the risks (Figure 9.6).

Treat Schedule Compression Risks

There are many types of risk treatment actions like risk prevention and mitigation, avoidance, transfer, and acceptance. Risk treatment (ISO 31000 Risk Management) is sometimes called risk response (PMBOK Guide). Schedule optimization is often an elusive exercise in risk management to find the "sweet spot" or balancing act between too much risk management that can constrain teams and not enough resulting in an unsuccessful project. Indeed, schedule optimization and risk management should be tuned to be continuous and concurrent in a fluid project environment. Schedule optimization techniques vary and are categorized as general, technical, and nontechnical.

First, general schedule optimization techniques include risk management, open communications, on-site and full-time workers, lean change management processes, and so on that reduce risks and improve the probability of success not only for compressed schedule projects but for any complex project. A goal of project management maturity is to achieve the right maturity level appropriate for the project considering schedule compression risks.

Second, schedule compression techniques (Table 8.1) are often mathematical simulations to optimize the schedule and budget (e.g., minimize schedule time and costs). Apply mathematical schedule compression techniques during the project planning phase when projects are underway (adkAr). These mathematical simulations have been called a "tedious and difficult task" (Salhab et al. 2023, 4) and require specialized competencies (e.g., schedule compression and optimization modeling skills, knowledge, and experience). Advanced scheduling is an out-of-scope topic for this book as the focus is on pre-project activities (e.g., the front-end of ADKar change management).

Third, some schedule compression risks can be treated through non-technical means like using overdesign and/or early release tactics:

Overdesign: to provide "more" than may be required by adding a safety margin should the requirements change. For example, bigger, stronger, faster, lighter, and longer are design factors that may reduce risk like purchasing a little bit more quantum computing time in the cloud than may be required. However, project costs (e.g., materials and labor) are likely to increase due to treating risks with overdesign decisions. Use the overdesign tactic early in the project and collaborate with the procurement team and especially if these items are long-lead time purchases.

Early Release: to release preliminary information early to downstream activities to reduce sensitivity risks. The risk is that an upstream activity may change resulting in some rework in downstream activities. Thus, low- and moderate-risk activities (activities 2, 3, and 4; Figure 8.3) may be candidates for early release.

Due to the possibility the design changes, the probability of rework is usually higher with an early release than an overdesign approach. However, if the project priority is to minimize time and not cost, then overdesign may be a better schedule optimization approach for some work packages. Both overdesign and early release tactics can be combined and applied.

Mitigate any schedule delays by injecting additional resources (e.g., schedule crashing) to bring the project back to the approved schedule if a speedy completion remains the project priority. Again, use the risk register to document the risk treatment actions and identify team members who are delegated prevention and mitigation responsibilities. Monitor the risks with the risk register to ensure treatment actions are sufficiently implemented and risk and issues are under control (prevented, mitigated, and resolved).

Monitor and Control Schedule Compression Risks

Once prevention and mitigation treatment actions have been or are being implemented, the project team monitors and controls risks and issues.

The purpose of monitoring is to track project progress, confirm risk treatment is effective, identify any variances, and adjust to control the variances. Monitoring is ongoing with informal techniques to gain insights like asking a team member how things are going or if they need to work any overtime. Approved project schedules usually do not resource above an accepted number of hours per week; team members working above this hours per week threshold is often an "error message" of compressed schedule issues.

Monitoring can be more formal with weekly risk management status meetings for tighter control. Project and program risk management may interface with the organization's broader risk management framework. Enterprise risk management includes monitoring project risks and operational risks (pre-project and post-project phases). The NIST (2020) Enterprise Risk Management Framework NISTIR 8286 guides the reader to take an organization-wide approach to risk management including monitoring. Here, monitoring is continuous and iterative: monitor, analyze, and control for effective governance of risks.

In the construction industry, there is a general agreement that these advanced and high-risk techniques require close monitoring and control due to the low success rate of schedule compression methods. For instance, Salhab (2023) and her research team found these techniques were successful only 21.4 percent of the time, implying most projects in the sample failed due to severe risks becoming impactful issues! However, other project teams were able to optimize schedules like in the Wuhan hospital construction projects. Clearly, projects are unique and applying schedule compression techniques is not guaranteed to be successful but can be when done right. Therefore, the monitor and control actions of risk management are crucial in schedule compression projects. The team specifically monitors that treatment actions (e.g., prevention and mitigation) are implemented as planned. The risk status changes from green to amber should the team struggle to treat risks and then to red if the risks are out of control for the team (e.g., they lack sufficient resources to treat the risk without an approved change request).

The projects and initiatives to adopt quantum technologies and transition to quantum safe cryptography can take a decade or more. A decade of projects can result in project fatigue; therefore, be proactive and prevent project fatigue, rather than mitigating it:

- Set realistic project and sprint pacing,
- Communicate regularly the case for change,
- Get senior leadership involved on a regular basis,
- Recognize the efforts and the emotional journey of project team members,
- Monitor project fatigue indicators like a drop in engagement or an increase in conflict and complaints,
- Give your teams a break and plan for slowing down to allow for leave and celebrations,
- And of course, implement best practices for project teams like decentralized decision making and risk taking.

Strategic initiatives and day-to-day operations lend themselves to metrics to improve monitoring. Hence, when developing the schedule compression strategy, identify the metrics that are critical to monitor like earned value project performance metrics. Earned value monitoring mathematically compares the planned value of work, actual cost, and earned value of work completed to evaluate project progress, cost efficiency, and schedule performance and then make any necessary adjustments (control).[39]

Quantum technology projects, especially schedule compression projects, benefit from mature project monitoring, control and risk management with performance metrics (e.g., earned value analysis). For successful schedule compression, start with a well-planned strategy that is developed, implemented, and monitored; otherwise, project teams will face greater uncertainty and risks.

Schedule Compression Best Practices and Recommendations

Reviewing the schedule compression research, there are obvious best practices and recommendations to apply and tailor to quantum technology

---

[39]We leave it to the reader to investigate earned value analysis to determine if this advanced project performance technique is appropriate for their projects.

projects. To organize these best practices, they have been grouped into familiar people, processes, and technologies categories. Schedule compression planning, contracting, and implementing recommendations are also reviewed.

People Best Practices

Quantum technology projects are completed by people; therefore, where it makes sense, resource the compressed schedule project with dedicated full-time project staff that are at the project site and empowered to make quick decisions. Reduce the number of project team members who have commitments to other projects or to operational KPIs (e.g., incident resolution time commitments) that may result in critical resources unexpectedly deprioritizing quantum project work. Of course, these rarefied project specialists are also great working in teams and may appreciate joining earlier in the project rather than later (e.g., a best practice in concurrent engineering where SMEs collaborate early in the project resulting in improved quality).

Competent people: For schedule compression strategies and tactics to work, begin with the right people on the project; that is, recruit people who are competent in schedule compression projects. Go beyond technical skills like understanding the mechanics of schedule compression theory and look for a compression mindset that values open and transparent communication, a commitment to project objectives and a propensity to develop empathetic, collaborative, and positive working relations for the intricate work ahead. They have the personal trait of acting with a sense of urgency. These effective project team competencies can be planned, modeled, and nurtured. For instance, workshops using Gizmos are also team-building opportunities. For this reason, layer team-building best practices with project workshops to strengthen ADKar change management.

Global shortage: However, there is a global shortage of quantum technology SMEs that may require organizations to develop quantum talent from within. Organizations can introduce *learn by doing activities* (e.g., experiment with quantum algorithms in a quantum "playpen") to help upskill internal teams. Learn by doing is like active learning in the adult education community and can increase a person's quantum competencies. Leaders reinforce and provide learn by doing opportunities; they are planned into the change management project (ADKar, adkAr, and adkaR phases) and into annual personnel development plans supported with quantum technologies learning resources.

Schedule compression values: Since values drive behavior and decision making, review the project's values and tune them for schedule compression projects like adaptability, accountability, and risk oriented. Indeed, the original Agile Manifesto values (e.g., collaboration) and principles (e.g., continuous attention to technical excellence and design) apply to compressed schedule projects. Values go beyond being printed and read; instead, they are action oriented and modeled by leadership (formal and informal leaders).

Effective teams: A best practice in successful compressed schedule projects is team integration where work progresses relatively smoothly between plan, design, procure, build, and quality control phases. Subsystem integration with multiple project teams occurs with minimal handovers or change requests. These integrated teams are high-performing because the members have sufficient schedule compression competencies. For example, they have and apply basic *knowledge* of fast tracking and crashing theory (e.g., they may have a professional certification in project management that includes scheduling content). They may also have *experience* in other compressed schedule projects that contributed to their compressed schedule *skills* development. Thus, compression schedule competence includes compression schedule knowledge, skills, and experience that are effectively applied (Figure 5.1). These team members are also competent with regular project activities like paying on time, proactively engaging with stakeholders and making timely updates and decisions. Indeed, recruit the best you can find is a critical success factor for "flash track" projects (Austin 2016, 9).

Supportive project culture: A supportive project culture within the people category of schedule compression best practices is another critical success factor. The project culture includes typical best practices like open communications and effective teams. There is high trust and managed risk taking. The integrated team is action oriented, adaptive, collaborative, and cooperative. There are servant leaders including the project leadership (internal and external leadership). These include executive leadership, the project sponsor and champions (See Figure 10.3, discussed later).

Desire and commitment: Build a strong desire to succeed and a "can-do" attitude to drive quantum technology projects (desire and commitment), by fostering a culture of urgency. Building and sustaining this attitude is essential for program success and aligns with the AD-KAR change management model. A critical success factor in compressed schedule projects is empowering teams to cocreate and take ownership of their tasks. To effectively implement a schedule compression strategy, team-based execution is crucial—fast-paced projects rely on well-formed, high-performing teams. The extensive body of knowledge on effective teamwork and bottom-up strategies provides additional insights into this people-focused approach should the reader wish for more information.

To conclude this section, people remain central to project success. Even with the right tools and techniques, it is ultimately team collaboration that determines how effectively complex strategies are implemented. Leaders must foster a culture of trust, shared ownership, and continuous learning—conditions that strengthen communication and reduce risk and build desire and commitment. A strong collaborative environment also enables teams to cocreate viable solutions, adapt quickly to change, and apply advanced delivery strategies with confidence.

This people-first foundation is critical when transitioning to process-based best practices. A strategy-driven compressed schedule approach demands the use of techniques such as fast tracking, crashing, concurrent engineering, and earned value management. However, their effective application relies not just on a technical understanding but on the maturity of the organization's risk, project, and service management practices and processes.

Process Best Practices

Lean processes are critical for compressed schedule success; the goal is to eliminate or at least reduce process "pain points" and to achieve an optimal end-to-end process completion time (e.g., integrated plan, design, procure, build, test, go-live, and close out phases). The goal is to develop lean processes and work interfaces that reduce variability and uncertainty and to optimize output predictability (e.g., sufficient quality).

The retail innovator IKEA excels with simple tools and process diagrams to assemble ("build") their products. Consider the result (project deliverables) if the step-by-step instructions (the process) were missing and the resulting quality issues. How long would it take to assemble the IKEA product without the process diagram? How much rework would result? Therefore, optimize the project, service, and change management processes for the many quantum technologies projects to follow (Figure 4.1).

When processes are lean and automated, risks are reduced and achieving quality targets are more likely. Despite lean project processes, there may still be risks to project work as compressed work moves through processes. For this reason, map out the key processes for the quantum technology project and manage their risks. Build risk prevention actions into the schedule for any severe schedule compression process risks. Lean processes often reflect a shallow hierarchy; therefore, identify and manage any risks related to "bloated" processes in hierarchical structures (e.g., multiple approvals are required).

Finally, aim for lean project procurement processes that can greatly contribute to compressed schedule success. Often, progress lags in the build phase if there are procurement disruption issues. Consequently, many compressed schedule projects benefit from procurement process optimization integrated with risk management. Achieve further optimization with the reverse design method to reduce procurement and supply chain risks. Prioritize long-lead time items for early funding and procurement. A lean procurement process allows the project team to select and approve contracts and deliverables on time. Add design-freeze points to the schedule to guide procurement decisions and reduce risks. Support project procurement processes with technology best practices (e.g., AI and automation).

Technology Best Practices

The project and construction management community learned from the Wuhan hospital compressed schedule projects and technology played a significant role in project success. BIM software was used that brings together multidisciplinary project data from the plan phase through to when the asset is handed over and used in operations. Therefore, use software that integrates the project plan, design, build, quality control, transition to production, go-live, closure activities through to technology operations (e.g., ITIL Service Management). Integrated project software improves decision making with real-time project information especially for evolution and sensitivity insights into overlapping activities. Look for competent team members who have experience with these technologies on compressed schedule projects.

In addition to best practices in schedule construction regarding people, processes, and technologies, there are recommendations in other critical activities grouped into planning, contracting, and implementing to apply to quantum technologies projects with compressed schedules.

Planning Recommendations

There are many project schedule compression planning recommendations from construction projects (e.g., the Wuhan COVID-19 hospital construction best practices) that apply to quantum technology projects. Schedule compression projects benefit from planning—lots of it and with internal and external teams. Whatever type of planning—rolling wave, continual, midterm, and short-term planning—it continues throughout the project to advance work, reduce risks, and ensure integration with seamless and predictable handovers. Activity monitoring and planning are ongoing throughout the compressed schedule project.

Researchers consistently conclude that successful compression projects featured risk-based planning. As teams progress through the project, risk management permeates and activity adjustments are made to prevent and mitigate risks, resulting in a higher probability of compression schedule success. Look for opportunities to use artificial intelligence and automation technologies (e.g., substitution) in compressed schedule projects.

Contracting Recommendations

There are many contracting recommendations from compressed schedule projects that can be applied to quantum technology projects. Due to complex contracting processes and systems in some organizations, there is a risk that the contract approval process may face delays, resulting in delays to subsequent project phases. Hence, review and tune the contracting process for quantum technology projects; that is, reduce pain points and approval turnaround times. Additionally, update procurement policies and procedures to align with updated quantum technology strategies (e.g., do not purchase quantum-vulnerable technologies).

Given the complexity of fast track projects and their associated risks, tailor contracts early in the project for crucial work such as procuring long-lead-time equipment or onboarding key people. Explore alternative contracts like partnering agreements (e.g., share risks and rewards) that align contracting parties to manage risk. Finally, tailor contracts to be lean (e.g., not too much and not too little content). When contracting processes are lean and optimized, it is more likely that timely contract approvals and change requests are achieved. Tune contracts and the contracting process for quantum technologies and services during the technical maturity optimization projects (Figure 1.2).

Implementing Recommendations

Finally, apply, tailor, and combine schedule compression best practices to quantum technology projects during implementing phases. Implementing is doing project work whether it be in the plan, design, build, test, or go-live phases. Embed the quantum compressed schedule strategies in the project plan to guide project work. Schedule compression projects benefit from the same implementation best practices as regular projects like a focus on risk and communications management to keep work progressing. Implementing teams also follow optimized processes (e.g., the project change control process). Despite mature processes, manage risks as they can quickly lead to compression schedule issues (e.g., risks are realized and converted into issues).

Schedule compression projects benefit from information like KPIs, often in real time to guide decision making and can be found in risk registers and other project systems. Improve effective control for fast track projects with mature practices like earned value calculations that allow deeper insights into project, schedule, and budget performance. Therefore, the project team identifies, designs, and baselines project performance KPIs in the planning phase aligned to the project priority and used in subsequent project performance reporting.

Since schedule compression projects are inherently risky, often with high uncertainty, they may provide overly challenging work at times, especially in the testing and the transition to production project phases. So, look after project teams and provide decisive and servant leadership. Schedule and conduct regular team building throughout the implementation (e.g., proof of concept testing with lunch). The team is resourced with competent A-list talent and looking after these quantum SMEs is just smart practice!

Integrate quantum technologies using the ITIL Service Management framework to guide their end-to-end application across business, technology, and cybersecurity domains. By aligning with this widely accepted framework (or COBIT), organizations reduce risk and increase the likelihood of achieving the required level of quality. Start your quantum journey by developing ITIL-aligned strategies that incorporate quantum technologies from the outset.

If schedule compression becomes necessary, use ITIL practices to design a structured compression strategy. Apply best practices across people, processes, and technologies—as well as planning, contracting, and executing recommendations—to improve the probability of compression schedule success. Use advanced techniques like fast tracking, crashing, and substitution only if your team has the required competence. These methods significantly increase risk, and demand high levels of project management maturity. As Lu et al. (2023, 3699) state, they are "not easy to implement, leading to significant challenges on all fronts." Allocate sufficient time during the strategy (ADKar) and planning (adkAr) phases to perform the sophisticated analysis and simulations required for a realistic and achievable compressed schedule. Take deliberate action now to build the capacity and foresight needed for successful quantum project delivery.

Managing a compressed schedule for quantum technology projects is a challenging task; however, by integrating risk management, the probability of success increases. Specifically, follow a process to evaluate the competencies of the team and capabilities of the organization to compress the project schedule. Develop and implement the compressed schedule strategy following a risk management approach. Apply schedule compression best practices and follow recommendations regarding people, process, technology, planning, contracting and implementing to deliver the compressed schedule.

Microlearning

Managing the quantum compressed schedule strategy may be daunting; however, since schedule compression strategies and tactics have long been studied, there are many online resources to extend your learning:

- Find out about relationship contracts (e.g., forbearance and reciprocity as in partnering and alliance agreements) that may be an improvement upon traditional (tight) procurement contracts that allow for more flexibility,
- Learn about schedule compression strategies and case studies in your industry and discipline,
- Find out about advanced scheduling certifications that include topics about compressed schedules best practices.

CHAPTER 10

Driving Accelerated Quantum Technologies Change

> *Do the impossible, because almost everyone has told me my ideas are merely fantasies.*
> Howard Hughes (Aviator and Record-Setter in Flight Speed)

The goal of *Accelerated Quantum Technologies Change Management* is to provide a framework for the front-end of change management leading to the approval for quantum technology projects, whether for a full program or beginning with just a quantum awareness initiative. The purpose of this chapter is to expedite the pre-project (ADKar) steps with a guided writing approach: the change management plan begins with strategy and with the first sentence or a list of bullets. Just start writing is the advice for those who desire a quick start to their quantum journey. Some may have "analysis paralysis" and delay putting "pen to paper" perhaps because they want a bit more information about quantum computing; just start writing down your thoughts as you read this chapter.

To accelerate the front-end of change management, begin with a strategy and document its contents however rough it may be. Over time and cocreation iterations with quantum stakeholders, the strategy evolves until it is endorsed and approved. To achieve approval to proceed with the program of quantum technology projects (Figure 1.2), the quantum champions progress through the ADKar change management process beginning with strategy development.

Getting a Quick Start: ADKar

Two key strategies are developed for an ADKar quick start: begin the overall quantum technology strategy (Chapter 3) and a short-term ADKar change management plan. The short-term plan is designed to overcome barriers and to begin the journey to initiate a quantum technologies program of projects (Figure 4.1). Structure a 100-day plan with three phases for a quick start—prepare, manage accelerated change, and sustain 100-day outcomes Figure 10.1). The chapter concludes with the ADKar 100-day change management plan to guide your writing and to accelerate the organization's quantum journey.

The prepare, accelerate, and sustain phases of the accelerated change management plan are described next.

Figure 10.1 Three-phase accelerated change management for quantum technologies

Prepare the ADKar Change Management Approach

Use the following content to guide your quick start to quantum technologies change management by adding headings and bullets to your own document. Start with a lessons learned exercise about previous change management projects (Figure 10.1). Then, develop the overall quantum technologies strategy and 100-day plan.

Lessons learned: What actions should the organization *stop* doing that did not work well in other change management projects, what should it *continue* to do since it can help to accelerate change, and what should it *start* doing to accelerate change, break through barriers, and adopt quantum technologies? Consider these lessons learned as strategy is being developed.

Quantum strategy: To accelerate the front-end of a program of quantum technology projects (Figure 1.2) implement the ADKar strategy as outlined in Chapter 3 if not already in progress. Progressively elaborate the business, technology, and cybersecurity strategies for the quantum journey (Figures 3.4 and 3.6). Begin a gap analysis of the current and target states and develop the vision, goals, and a strategy to get there. Start a list of success criteria (see Chapter 7) for the quantum innovation and cybersecurity program of change and incorporate them into the organization's strategies and plans. The quantum technologies gap analysis should consider both their dual potentialities: bringing innovation through quantum technologies to the organization and its customers and migrating to quantum-safe cryptography. Finally, list the effects of not adopting quantum technologies on the organization including the risk of a quantum cyber-attack. These strategy elements (Table 10.1) form the basis for a quantum technologies communications plan and, if required, for the 100-day strategy.

Refer to this table when creating an infographic or FAQ for your organization's quantum technologies strategic outlook to achieve consistent messaging.

Sponsorship plan: Begin developing a plan for (i) sustainable sponsorship and (ii) sustainable funding. It may only be a paragraph or a page or two. Sponsorship might include two or more people, such as the CEO and a C-suite executive, who can provide both types of sponsorship.

Table 10.1 **Quantum technologies strategic outlook**

Dual Potentialities of quantum technologies		
Element	**Quantum innovation**	**Quantum-safe cryptography**
Vision	Add the vision for how quantum technologies adoption will enable new and optimized products and services.	Add the vision for how post-quantum cryptography and achieving cryptographic agility will benefit the organization.
Goals	Identify the top three goals for quantum technologies adoption such as creating a quantum technologies experimentation area or quantum business case development.	Identify the top three goals for becoming safe from a cryptographically-relevant quantum computer like updating procurement policies and procedures to halt purchasing cryptographically vulnerable technologies.
Rationale	Develop a concise rationale for adopting quantum technologies such as to provide new products and services (e.g., market disruption).	List the rationale for protecting the organization's data and systems from a hacker with a cryptographically-relevant quantum computer with new cryptography.
Success Criteria	Use the adoption determinants (Figure 7.2) to speed up quantum awareness, desire, and knowledge components for quantum technologies-driven innovation.	Use the adoption determinants (Figure 7.2) to speed up quantum awareness, desire, and knowledge components for post-quantum cryptographic migrations and cryptographic agility.
Effects of not adopting quantum technologies	Identify the effects of what happens if the organization does not adopt quantum technologies like losing market share to competitors.	Explain the effects of a quantum cybersecurity attack such as regulatory penalties, reputation damage and loss of market share.

Developing a sponsorship plan is improved when the sponsor–project champion dynamics are considered and discussed later in this chapter. The sponsorship plan will include content from the quantum technology strategies, training, communications, and risk management plans. Again, develop plans to achieve sponsorship goals to (i) receive approval to proceed with the ADKar process; (ii) create quantum technologies awareness for their dual potentialities; (iii) nurture a desire for the program of quantum technology projects; and (iv) develop sufficient knowledge to approve, fund, and initiate the organization's program of quantum technology projects.

Communications plan: develop an effective communications plan to accelerate progress through the ADKar phases by fostering quantum technologies awareness and engagement. Successful communications are planned, managed, controlled, and continuously improved with feedback and handling objections. Given the priority and urgency of adopting quantum technologies, get communications right to avoid delays. A structured communications approach enhances quality and reduces risk.

Develop a lean ADKar communications plan that includes the following:

1. **Stakeholder engagement:** identify key stakeholders and engagement strategies to help manage any resistance and to build desire;
2. **Communication goals and strategies:** establish clear communication objectives and required resources (e.g., a frequently asked questions document) related to ADKar;
3. **Content:** include curated information specific to the organization about the dual potentialities of quantum technologies to create awareness, desire, and knowledge;
4. **Communication channels:** select appropriate ways to communicate;
5. **Communication schedule:** provide status updates and feedback opportunities (e.g., polls);
6. **Roles and responsibilities:** assign communication tasks using a RACI[40] chart.

While there is more to project communications planning, addressing these five areas provides a lean start; tailor or generate additional content as necessary.

Upskilling plan: Another barrier to quantum technologies adoption is the lack of competencies. To resolve this issue, organizations can develop an upskilling program tailored for different stakeholders. Skulmoski and Walker (2023) in *Cybersecurity Training* outline upskilling strategies and learning initiatives for emerging technologies. By offering clear learning

---

[40]A project management tool that clarifies roles and responsibilities. RACI: Responsible, Accountable, Consulted, and Informed.

pathways, organizations can reduce resistance and build confidence in stakeholders.

Upskilling takes many forms from self-directed reading about change management (e.g., this book) to mentoring, training, and education. Mentoring is a developmental relationship in which an experienced individual shares insights to support the personal and professional growth of the other person. It is an ongoing partnership that fosters knowledge transfer, helping the quantum technologies mentee manage risks, build competence, and expand their perspective about the dual potentialities of quantum technologies.

Training goes beyond mentoring by providing structured, short-term learning to equip individuals with the knowledge and skills needed to adopt and apply quantum technologies. Training may include predefined content, hands-on practice, and working with practical use cases. Training may be offered internally or through external institutions like universities and vendors, which provide diverse learning pathways such as microcredentials and online courses. Universities typically provide education programs.

Risk management plan: projects and change initiatives fail when risks become significant issues, derailing success. Therefore, there are two risk management plans to develop: (i) a risk management plan for the overall ADKar change management plan and (ii) a risk management plan for the 100-day quantum technologies change management plan. Begin risk planning and conduct risk assessments for each plan and element (e.g., communications plan). Prioritize and manage any sponsorship and funding risks to accelerate the pre-project phase. Ensure a structured approach by following best practices like risk management (Figure 9.6) to reduce the time through the ADKar steps.

Perhaps a key risk is resistance to change. Address any resistance to adopting quantum technologies by first listening to stakeholders (strategic, tactical, and operational). Sometimes, hesitant adopters just want to be heard before accepting change. Address objections by distinguishing "what" needs to change from "how" to change it. Tailor standard messaging (e.g., failure to adopt PQC leaves systems vulnerable to quantum-based attacks) to individual concerns (e.g., strategic). Indeed, learn from successful salespeople who skillfully "handle objections" (e.g., manage resistance to change) to close the deal (e.g., get approval to proceed). Prevent and mitigate these risks through collaboration with others at the strategic and tactical levels.

When the individual 100-day plans in the prepare phase (Figure 10.1) are sufficiently developed, then integrate them into a holistic plan, implement, and manage the plan. Recall the aim is to quickly advance awareness, desire, and knowledge of the program of quantum technology projects with influential stakeholders and is made possible by following the integrated 100-day plan.

Manage Accelerated Change

The purpose of this phase is to accelerate the change management process (ADKar) with influential stakeholders. The key activities in the manage accelerated change phase (Figure 10.2) are to implement the change management plans from the prepare phase. There may be two streams of work: the overall ADKar change management activities and a 100-day plan to accelerate the front-end of change (Figure 10.2). The early and draft version of the strategy are under version control using the numbering 0.1, 0.2, 0.3, and so on until the draft version is endorsed and then approved. The approved version numbering for the quantum technologies strategy

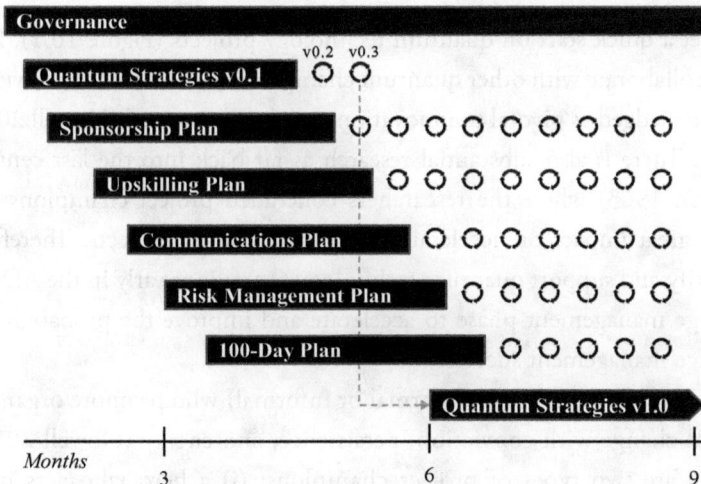

Figure 10.2 Accelerated quantum technologies Gantt chart

then changes to 1.0, 1.1, 1.2, and so forth when the version is updated through the project change control process (the dashed *dependency* line). The 100-day plan might not require formal approval other than by the CEO or another executive project sponsor.

Apply performance tracking to ensure change management activities are under control. Managing these plans is pure project management and we leave the reader to find additional information if required. Monitor the organization's ADKar progress with key stakeholders and adjust as necessary (Table 6.4).

Sustain ADKar Outcomes

In the sustain phase 3 for accelerated ADKar (Figure 10.1) continue to support and scale the awareness, desire, and knowledge for quantum technologies. There will be new joiners to convince as the organization progresses their quantum journey. For this reason, the ADKar phase for the quantum journey may be an iterative series of 100-day quantum strategy sprints (Figure 3.6). Of critical importance is to sustain sponsorship and program funding; the project champion role can be pivotal to the front-end including their relationship with executive sponsors.

Quantum Project Champions

To get a quick start on quantum technology projects (Figure 10.1), find and collaborate with other quantum champions as champions are "widely acknowledged as pivotal to innovation speed and success." (Howell 2005, 108). There is also substantial research as far back into the last century (Schon 1963) where the researchers concluded project champions can have great impact on accelerating the front-end of projects. Therefore, identify and support quantum technology champions early in the ADKar change management phase to accelerate and improve the probability of change management success.

Champions are leaders (formal or informal) who promote organizational change with conviction, persistence, and energy (Howell 2005). There are two types of project champions: (i) a hero who acts individually to promote the project, and (ii) collective champions where individuals collaborate with other like-minded people to work toward organizational change.

An early action for quantum champions is to identify the different types of quantum stakeholders (Figure 10.3) including strategic partners who can help develop sustained sponsorship and program funding. Executive leadership support (strategic) for technology change management projects has long been a change management critical success factor and perhaps the most important (Young and Jordan 2008). Strategic sponsors have enough power and resources to break through initial status quo barriers and sustain the change. Other sustaining sponsors—tactical—are closer to the quantum technology projects like a director of manufacturing and can sustain daily change momentum (Pádár et al. 2017). The initiating and sustaining sponsors may change over the life cycle of the quantum program of projects.

Quantum technologies change management (ADKar) is tailored for each group of stakeholders since they benefit from similar messages and may face similar types of quantum barriers. Strategic stakeholders may focus on financial barriers to adopting quantum technologies, while tactical stakeholders may be concerned about competency gaps. Monitor ADKar progress and status (Table 6.4) for quantum stakeholders.

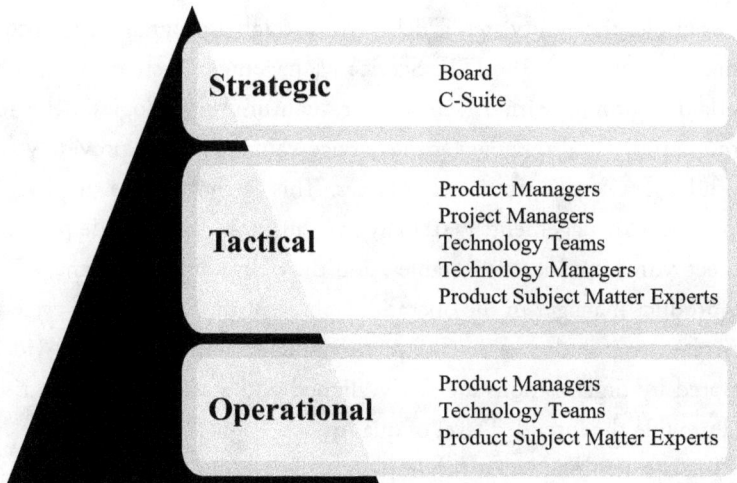

Strategic
Board
C-Suite

Tactical
Product Managers
Project Managers
Technology Teams
Technology Managers
Product Subject Matter Experts

Operational
Product Managers
Technology Teams
Product Subject Matter Experts

Figure 10.3 Strategic, tactical, and operational stakeholders

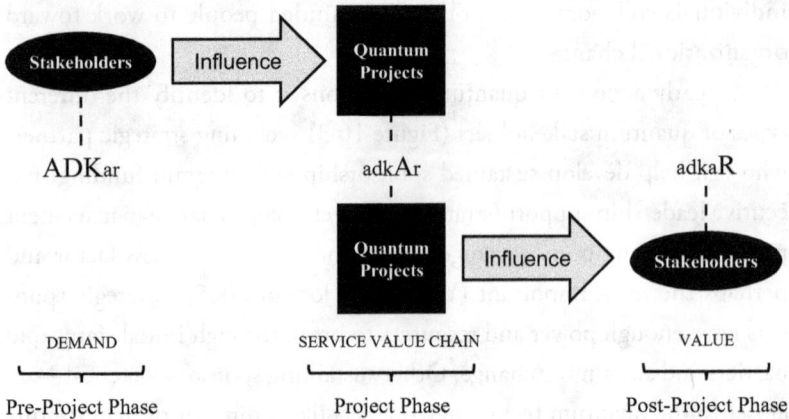

ADKAR Change Management: *Awareness – Desire – Knowledge – Ability – Reinforcement*

Figure 10.4 Quantum project stakeholder relationships

While the change and project management interplay of stakeholders (Figure 10.4) may appear complex, there are influential stakeholders like manufacturing leadership who can champion quantum technology projects and stakeholders like manufacturing engineers who are influenced by quantum deliverables. The project boundaries (Project Management Institute 2017a, 562) are also seen here including the pre-project, project, and post-project phases.

The ADKAR phases can also be included, as illustrated in Figure 10.4; for example, the ability step is delivered through a program of quantum technology projects. The ITIL Service Management System can also be overlaid beginning with a Demand for quantum technologies, delivered through projects also known as the Service Value Chain, to provide Value to end users of quantum technologies. This is the essence of product and project management: A strategy and business case precede projects; project teams produce deliverables, and the deliverables are managed by the product manager in the operations phase of the product life cycle to generate the intended value. The many standards and frameworks widely adopted by organizations are easily aligned and stacked to reduce risks and provide the intended level of quality.

We are reminded that "championing is a complex performance of contextually dependent collective social interaction, varying over time, rather than a heroic act of one individual promoting an idea" (van Laere and Aggestam 2016, 47). Quantum champions develop effective relationships with many types of stakeholders to progress change management. Change management is a team-based activity including forming a team beginning with strategic and tactical leadership.

Champion—Leadership Relationship

Leadership engagement and visible support are critical success factors for change management projects especially when a quick start is required. Leaders authorize, fund, and charter change management projects like those involving quantum technologies. Leaders can help others make sense of the changes brought about by quantum technologies. The type of relationship between the project champion and leadership is critical for project success. Controls too tight (e.g., lack of delegated decision making for the champion) can result in a constrained work effort. However, insufficient control can lead to undesired actions by the project champion. Hence, each organization and change project has a "sweet spot" of champion empowerment balanced with executive oversight (Kelley and Lee 2010).

In our books, the "Goldilocks Principle" can also be applied to change management projects: not too much of something (e.g., standards, processes, and governance) nor too little—just the right amount for a lean approach to achieve the required change objectives. As the levels of criticality, complexity, priority, and urgency increase (like in quantum technology projects), leadership oversight and engagement will likely increase to assist with risk management. Leadership can support champions visibly and regularly and celebrate their achievements.

Champion Identification

Project champions stand out and are often easy to identify. Their champion competencies are critical for change management success (van Laere and Aggestam 2016). They are respected by their peers throughout the organization and by external teams as well. They have a strong network relevant to the scope of the change project. They have complementary technical competencies (e.g., quantum algorithm programming and/ or business case development). They are servant leaders with the right amount of charisma, so the change focus is aligned with project and organizational goals rather than the change agent themselves. This implies they are great at fostering teams and in other ways of working like leading a quantum community of practice. They have communication skills that are tuned to ADKar change management; for instance, they are effective communicators, write and present well. They work with a sense of urgency and are known to be innovative.

These champions are adept at product and project management and are familiar with relevant frameworks (e.g., ITIL Service Management) and standards (ISO 31000 Risk Management). Champions have a way with supporting innovation initiatives that are aligned with the organization's vision and goals and stay away from "weak" initiatives (e.g., a natural filtering mechanism where weak projects are less likely to attract champions, Bertels et al. 2020). It is no surprise that effective change management champions are easy to identify—they are superstars!

Champions Can Remove Barriers

Champions are widely acknowledged as critical to change management velocity and success as they can overcome organizational inertia or fierce resistance to change. When faced with resistance, effective champions focus on the opportunities of the change (e.g., new materials development with quantum computing) rather than the threats of not changing (e.g., lose market share to competitors disrupting the market with new materials made possible with quantum computing and innovation).

One way to quickly gain momentum is to create a 100-day plan to progress ADKar change management. The 100-day plan requires a change management champion and a strategy for change.

ADKar 100-Day Plan

The ADKar 100-day plan is a subset of the main ADKar quantum technologies change management strategy and designed to quickly progress the quantum journey and proceed through the awareness, desire, and knowledge phases. A period of 100 days is only a guideline; be lean and make it 99 days or innovative with a 50+50 plan. Our approach is to apply, tailor, and combine standards and frameworks as we have in this book. Thus, apply this ADKar 100-day plan, tailor it to your needs, and combine with other content as necessary. Again, take the guided writing approach: Read, then write to create your own ADKar 100-day plan.

A goal of the 100-day plan is to create awareness, excitement, desire, commitment, and genuine engagement in the program of quantum technology projects for key stakeholders like senior leadership and the CEO. The ADKar plans that comprise the 100-day plan can be progressively elaborated as more information becomes available and understanding increases during and after the 100 days.

Getting Started with the 100-Day Plan

Developing the overall change management strategy and 100-day plan can be concurrent activities in an accelerated approach. Develop a 100-day change management plan to generate quantum technologies awareness, desire, and knowledge. The quantum technologies change management strategy (Chapter 3) may already be underway. A key question for the overall strategy and the 100-day plan is where is the beginning of the organization's change management project? Is there zero awareness, desire, and knowledge in the organization? Is there some awareness, but little desire for the dual potentialities of quantum technologies?

List and prioritize the goals for the 100-day plan; what does the organization wish to accomplish? Raise awareness? Secure program funding? Here are some 100-day goals to consider:

- Start the sustainable funding dialog with the CEO for this prolonged program of projects,
- Establish a steering committee for the quantum program of projects,
- Continue the risk analysis process with other stakeholders (including the Mosca Theorem risk analysis) and develop treatment plans,

- Produce a one-page infographic charter for quantum technologies change management that can be reused throughout the ADKar process,
- Find other quantum technology champions, form coalitions, and further elaborate the quantum technology strategies,
- Create a quantum technologies community of practice or a cryptographic agility community of practice with internal and external stakeholders,
- Identify early wins ("low hanging fruit") like providing access to a quantum technologies "play pen" to learn and experiment with quantum technologies,
- Identify ways to scale and maintain momentum for change (ADKar cycle sprints) beyond the initial 100-day plan.

Goals form the basis for a 100-day quantum technologies change management plan. The goals you develop may need or benefit from prioritization, endorsement and approval depending on where the start is for the 100-day plan. The overall 100-day plan comprises individual plans like the sponsorship plan.

100-Day Quantum Technologies Sponsorship Plan

Plan to identify and develop sponsorship in the first 100 days. Ideally, the CEO and the C-suite are key sponsors who can bring others onto the project like establishing a steering committee. There are formal and informal paths to the CEO and there are others in your organization who can advise how to contact the CEO and executive leadership as there may be protocols involved. Identify and then develop an ADKar plan to cultivate project sponsors. The CEO may sponsor a full program of projects through to perhaps only an exploratory quantum technologies strategy.

100-Day Quantum Technologies Upskilling Plan

While there are many forms of upskilling, in an accelerated situation, consider mentoring for executive and board-level sponsors. Mentoring in a 100-day initiative can focus on the ADKar steps through to providing guidance and knowledge transfer to help the quantum technologies sponsor manage risks, build competence, and expand their perspective about the dual potentialities of quantum technologies. Add the upskilling opportunities to the one-page infographic change management charter developed during communications planning, design, and development activities. Provide a curated quantum technologies reading list that will interest your executive sponsors that raises their awareness, desire, and knowledge.

100-Day Quantum Technologies Communications Plan

There are two communications plans: (i) for the sponsors, and (ii) for other quantum champions and collaborators (e.g., strategic and tactical partners at this point, Figure 10.3). Both communications plans can be developed concurrently; however, it is likely the sponsor communications plan will be implemented first and, therefore, discussed here. At the heart of the communications plan is strategy (Table 10.1). From the quantum strategy, include the rationale to adopt these technologies and how the program of quantum technology projects align with the organization's strategy and direction. Explain the deliverables and benefits to the organization and teams resulting from the quantum technology projects. Identify the consequences and risks of delay or project failure. The 100-day communications plan includes content to quickly progress through ADKar steps for quantum technologies adoption.

1. **Target audience:** Identify the intended sponsors (Figure 10.3);
2. **Communication outcomes:** What do you want the sponsors to think or do after they interact with the communication's message? Review the technology adoption determinants (Figure 7.2) for comprehensive messaging. Review quantum technologies readiness (Table 7.2) for messaging priority and precision. To progress, make these messages action oriented like including a quantum technologies infographic for the receiver to review and provide feedback;
3. **Sender:** Select the sender for the messages; initially it may you or someone more senior in the organization to approach the CEO regarding sponsorship;

4. **Key messages:** Develop sponsor messages that facilitate and accelerate the ADKar process (e.g., provide the "what's in it for me"
message). Begin by developing messages for each ADKar phase
and tailor the message to the sponsors. See also the case for change
in the *Start Now Imperative* section (Chapter 5) when crafting
sponsorship messages for the dual potentialities of quantum
technologies;

5. **Communication channels:** Determine how to contact the sponsors
(both formally and informally);

6. **Frequency:** Determine when to contact the sponsors and how often;

7. **Budget, schedule and resources:** Develop a preliminary and high-
level budget and schedule for the program of quantum technology
projects. Use range estimates and rough order of magnitude estimates. Identify any required internal or external resources for the
program of projects (Figure 1.2).

A goal of the communications plan is to enable reuse of key elements. For
example, a quantum technologies change management infographic from
the 100-day plan can be repurposed to introduce the dual potentialities
of quantum technologies and their organizational impacts during new
employee onboarding.

100-Day Risk Management Plan

Proactively manage any 100-day risks (Figure 9.6) including barriers to
adopting quantum technologies and their dual potentialities. Review the
barriers to adopting quantum technologies (Chapter 5). Use the Quantum Technology Barriers to Adoption Gizmo (Table 5.1) to evaluate
any adoption barriers in your organization including any barriers your
sponsors may face. Document and manage any significant barriers as issues in the risk register.[41] Review the *Start Now Imperative* for reasons to
start the quantum journey and develop responses to barriers and to possible

---

[41]Be tactful and sensitive when writing risks and issues as a raised risk can offend
people if they are identified as the owner of a risk! Contact the prospective risk
owner prior to raising the risk in the risk register.

objections like the organization already has too much project work. Managing objections effectively brings the quantum champion closer to approval to proceed to develop a quantum strategy. Managing resistance to change and objections can be addressed in the communications and risk management plans.

Integrate The 100-Day Plans

Craft these elements together into an integrated 100-day plan. Add a scope statement and rationale, schedule, budget and risks and issues. There may be some type of approval to proceed with the 100-day plan that can be an early milestone. Combine the individual plans into an actionable 100-day plan that includes:

- **Project scope statement:** Detail the project's main deliverables, the delivery date and the 100-day budget if applicable. Some add assumptions and constraints;
- **Work breakdown structure:** Elaborate the 100-day strategy's scope in a WBS (Figure 10.5);

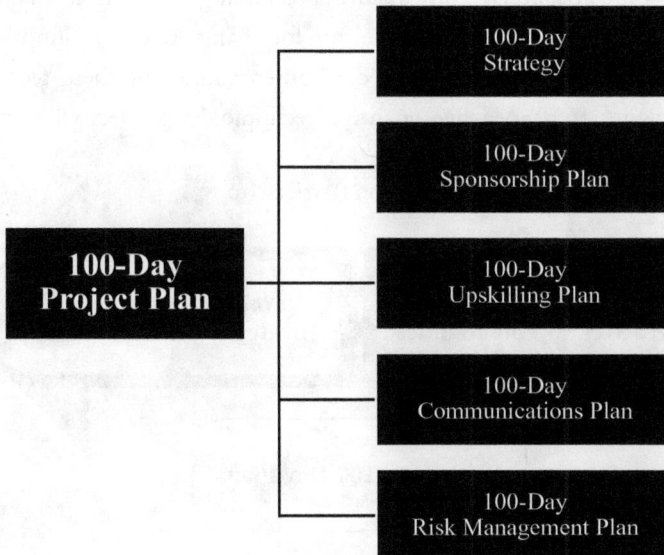

Figure 10.5 Hundred-day work breakdown structure

- **Project rationale:** the reason for the ADKar 100-day plan and the problems it addresses;
- **Schedule:** The ADKar 100-day schedule may be in many formats like a weekly checklist of items to complete, a Gantt chart through to a formal network diagram with 50 to 60 activities. Use the WBS as the input to develop the 100-day schedule;
- **Budget:** the funds and resources required to complete the ADKar 100-day plan; some 100-day initiatives might not require a budget;
- **Risks:** Follow the risk management process (Figure 9.6) to identify, analyze, and treat risks and issues that may interfere with the 100-day plan (e.g., there is a risk it may be difficult to meet with the CEO).

Implement the 100-day plan. Once approval to proceed is provided (if required), follow the schedule and act with a sense of urgency! A period of 100 days passes quickly. Use risk management and standard governance techniques to monitor and control the 100-day plan.

The ADKar 100-day plan is adaptive and responsive to change over the 100 days and beyond like agile plans should be. Indeed, there may be a series of 100-day plans that can be managed through a product backlog and sprints.

To conclude, accelerating quantum technologies adoption is a change management project. Identify the case for change that are found in the drivers and imperatives for the dual potentialities for these technologies (Figure 10.6). Manage quantum technologies barriers with change

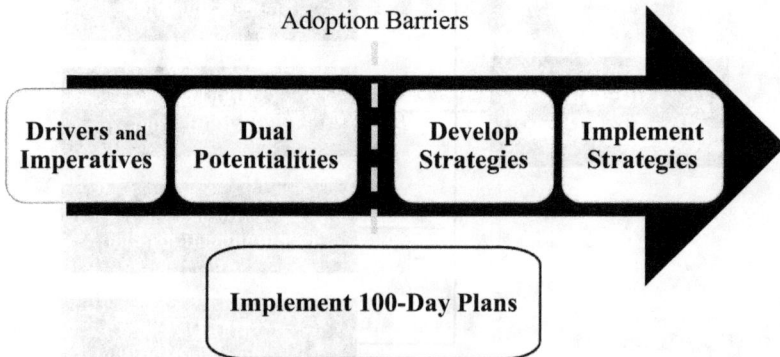

Figure 10.6 Accelerated quantum technologies change management approach

management techniques like a 100-day plan. The goal is to rapidly over-come quantum technology barriers and initiate adoption through strategic planning, followed by planning, implementing, and optimizing quantum technologies.

Good luck with your guided writing; it is truly an expedient way to develop strategies and plans.

Microlearning

There are many resources to accelerate projects and other activities related to change management. Find out more about:

- Relationship building with senior and executive leadership,
- Critical success factors or lessons learned for 100-day plans,
- The seven-step sales process to get approval to proceed,
- How to handle objections in a "selling" situation,
- How project champions succeed.

CHAPTER 11

Conclusion

> *Life begins at the end of your comfort zone.*
> Neale Donald Walsch

Since the United Nations declared 2025 to be the *International Year of Quantum Science and Technology*, there has been an increased awareness of the dual potentialities of quantum technologies. There are fabulous promises of innovation, new materials and breakthroughs in medicine; indeed, quantum-as-a-savior. However, there is a severe risk that a cryptographically-relevant quantum computer may be used by a hacker to steal the organization's data and/or disrupt its operations. But when? There is a lack of consensus; however, there is a risk that these technologies may arrive sooner than anticipated. While we may not know exactly when a cryptographically-relevant quantum computer will appear, we do know it is imperative to migrate to quantum-secure technologies like PQC from NIST.

There is unanimous advice and recommendations to migrate to PQC without delay because of the issue a cryptographically-relevant quantum computer will be able to "break" public-key encryption, compromising data security, digital signatures, and authentication; hackers will succeed with their objectives should it be to steal and/or disrupt. We detail a program-oriented approach in our previous book *Quantum Cybersecurity Program Management* (Skulmoski and Memari 2025a) that can be applied, tailored, and combined with other approaches to help accelerate quantum technologies implementation (adkAr). However, some organizations have not started their quantum journey and are in the pre-project phase of change management.

Given the criticality, complexity, priority, and urgency of adopting quantum technologies, begin with updating the business, technology, and cybersecurity strategies for quantum technologies including strengthening classical cybersecurity if required. Progressively elaborate until these strategies are approved and baselined. However, there are often quantum technology barriers to adoption resulting in organizations delaying the start of their quantum journey. Fortunately, there is a vast body of knowledge about breaking through barriers like using the ADKAR change management approach.

Use change management to create awareness, desire, and knowledge. Develop an ADKar 100-day plan to break through barriers to get permission to proceed with a program of quantum technology projects (Figure 1.2). Consider using a 100-day plan to accelerate the front-end of the change management project.

Should the organization need to catch up in a hurry, it is best to consider the feasibility of schedule compression in the pre-project phase to set realistic expectations for the project teams. Schedule compression is inherently risky, and the risks are likely to compound when applied to inherently risky technology projects (e.g., post-quantum cryptographic migrations, Figure 9.5). Perhaps the best way to compress a schedule is to start sooner but a great way to start is to use the headings in Table 10.1 to start writing. Use risk management (Figure 9.6) throughout and continuously.

Good luck with your quantum journey. No doubt it will be exciting. I wish I could be there with you as you are shepherding in a new era.

Sincerely

Greg

Gold Coast, Australia (2025)

Appendixes

An efficient way to collaborate and to progress the change management process is to bring together quantum champions and other subject matter experts to plan, implement, and optimize quantum technologies including post-quantum cryptographic migrations. Successful project managers and change champions use the workshop approach to bring together stakeholders to cocreate and to progress change management objectives. Next, is an introduction to workshop techniques and how to use Gizmos in the accelerated quantum technologies change management journey.

Workshop Management

Workshops are a form of cocreation in a group setting ranging from a few people to 50 or more. Workshops can bring team members through the ADKar change management process and improve their capabilities ahead of quantum technology projects. Workshops can improve the awareness, desire, and knowledge elements of change management and reduce resistance to change. Workshops are also commonly used in projects to engage and collaborate with stakeholders (e.g., design workshops to elicit and elaborate project requirements). While there are many workshop formats, the following can be used to kick off the quantum technologies awareness workshop:

Introduction—Senior leadership: quantum strategy and workshop goals,

Presentation—Transformative Capabilities of Quantum Technologies (use cases that may be considered by the organization),

Groupwork Activity—Apply to their business: Where can we optimize (minimize and maximize)? What are the benefits of optimizing? What can we simulate?

Lunch—Provide a special lunch to send the message that this work is important,

Presentation—Quantum Roadmap (business strategy update and quantum business case development, cybersecurity foundation, post-quantum cryptographic migrations) with the Gantt chart (Figure 4.1),

Discussion—What do we need to stop doing, continue doing, and start doing to get a quick start on the quantum pathway? What are the risks and issues?

Next Steps—What can we do in the next three weeks? What work can be initiated (e.g., ADKar initiatives and planning for the cryptographic discovery inventory project)?

Workshop Closure—Senior leadership's expectations and encouragement.

Sometimes workshops can result in identifying a quantum champion and quantum steering committee unless these roles are already assigned. A critical point is there is formality in the process and proceedings (e.g., minutes are taken, and the next steps are followed up). Recall that the very best talent are invited to bring quantum technologies to the organization, and they thrive with a high level of project and service management maturity. While this workshop was focused on developing awareness for quantum technologies, it could instead focus on schedule compression strategies, Gizmo analysis (next appendix) or managing post-quantum cryptographic risks using a similar structure and approach. Leverage the workshop as a team building exercise to maximize the event benefits.

Microlearning

Collaborating with others using the workshop approach is long regarded as best practice. Learn more about:

- How are *serious games* used in workshops to improve engagement,
- How to *park* out-of-scope discussions and continue engagement,
- Workshops by watching instructional videos about effective workshop management and team building,
- Making workshops action oriented.

Detailed Technical Maturity Capability Gizmos

Use the Detailed Technical Maturity Capability Gizmos to gain a deep and early understanding of the quantum technologies change management program of projects including the pre-project, project, and post-project phases. Rate and discuss, especially any variances and then put in place actions to progress. Technical maturity management is a stack of best practices including project, service, change, and cybersecurity management maturity: the *technical maturity stack*.

Detailed project management Gizmo	Rate, discuss, and act	Rating High Low
People	What is the level of project management competency for this organization or department and external teams?	5 4 3 2 1
Technology	What is the level of project management technology (e.g., software) capabilities for this organization/department and external teams?	5 4 3 2 1
Processes	What is the level of project management process maturity for this organization/ department and external teams?	5 4 3 2 1

Detailed service management Gizmo	Rate, discuss, and act	Rating High Low
People	What is the level of service management competency for this organization or department?	5 4 3 2 1
Technology	What is the level of service management technology (e.g., software) capabilities for this organization or department?	5 4 3 2 1
Processes	What is the level of service management process maturity for this organization or department?	5 4 3 2 1

Detailed change management Gizmo	Rate, discuss, and act	Rating High Low
People	What is the level of change management competency (e.g., Prosci ADKAR) for this organization or department?	5 4 3 2 1
	How much awareness is there for quantum?	5 4 3 2 1
	How much desire is there for quantum?	5 4 3 2 1
	How much knowledge is there for quantum?	5 4 3 2 1
Technology	What is the level of change management technology (e.g., software) capabilities for this organization or department?	5 4 3 2 1
	What is the level of change management tools (training and templates) for this organization or department?	5 4 3 2 1
Processes	What is the level of change management process maturity for this organization or department?	5 4 3 2 1

Detailed cybersecurity management Gizmo	Rate, discuss, and act	Rating High Low
People	What is the level of cybersecurity management competency for this organization or department and external partners?	5 4 3 2 1
Technology	What is the level of cybersecurity management technology (e.g., software) capabilities for this organization or department and external partners?	5 4 3 2 1
Processes	What is the level of cybersecurity management maturity for this organization or department and external partners?	5 4 3 2 1

Document any risks and issues in the risk register. Indeed, inform leadership about any severe risks or high impact issues. Update strategies and plans.

U.S. Defense Contract Management Agency Schedule Analyzer

The American Defense Contract Management Agency (DCMA) has developed a set of schedule analysis tools to ensure high quality and reliable project schedules. They developed a 14-point analysis guide to find defects in schedules (Defense Contract Management Agency 2005). This is a quality control procedure (find and fix defects) and is illustrated in Figure 9.7. To ensure high levels of quality when developing a compressed schedule, look for the following:

1. **Logic:** Ensure all tasks have logical relationships (e.g., finish-to-start, start-to-start);
2. **Leads:** Check for inappropriate use of lead time in activity relationships;
3. **Lags:** Evaluate whether lag time is appropriately applied in activity sequences;
4. **Relationship Types:** Determine the correct relationship types, particularly minimizing start-to-finish activities and maximizing finish-to-start activities;
5. **Hard Constraints:** Verify there is minimum use of hard date constraints, which can limit schedule flexibility;
6. **High Float:** Identify any tasks with excessive float, which may uncover issues with logic or scheduling;
7. **Negative Float:** Detect any negative float, which may point to scheduling conflicts or unrealistic deadlines;
8. **High Duration:** Highlight any activities with long durations that might be hiding scheduling issues;
9. **Invalid Dates:** Ensure activities have valid start and finish dates;
10. **Resources:** Verify that resources are appropriately allocated without overallocation;
11. **Missed Tasks:** Find any tasks that have been missed;
12. **Critical Path Test:** Ensure the critical path(s) is valid and accurately represented;
13. **Critical Path Length Index (CPLI):** Measure the efficiency and effectiveness of the critical path to meet project objectives;

14. **Baseline Execution Index (BEI):** Evaluate the degree the project is performing against approved schedule.

Like any tool or process, tailor and combine as required. Since managing a compressed schedule is continuous once approval to proceed out of the planning phase, schedule analysis is also continuous throughout the project. This DCMA quality control tool may also be used outside of the planning phase especially when crashing and overlapping activities in real time. Look for opportunities to add automation and AI capabilities to this analysis. As you can see, there is a lot to schedule creation, analysis and management.

Glossary

Our glossary is tailored to quantum cybersecurity. Purists may find we may have tailored our definitions a bit too much. Still, we take some liberty to tailor and combine to create an applied glossary for *Accelerated Quantum Technologies Change Management* for readers who are new to quantum technologies. The reader is encouraged to go online to find or generate additional information.

Algorithm: a set of instructions (e.g., a suite of quantum circuits) to solve a problem or perform calculations and can be thought of as software used by a quantum computer (hardware).

Capability: the effectiveness or maturity of the organization to plan, implement, and optimize their strategies (see *Competence*).

Classical cryptography: cryptography that is secure against classical computing but not quantum computers (see also *Post-quantum cryptography*).

Combine: bring together tools and processes from different standards and frameworks.

Competence: the knowledge skills and abilities that are effectively applied by the people on the project teams (see *Capability*).

Continual improvement: continuous improvement with deliberate activities to benchmark and bring in best practices; that is, improve and optimize continuously and look to external best practices to guide improvement.

Critical path: the sequence of dependent project activities that determines the earliest possible project completion date, where any delay directly delays the overall project completion.

Cryptographic agility: the ability to update the organization's cryptography efficiently and effectively (e.g., update only the algorithms rather than replace devices).

Cryptographically-relevant quantum computer: quantum technologies with sufficient capabilities to break public-key systems (e.g., asymmetric cryptography) used to protect systems with classical cryptography. Mosca's "Z" parameter represents the arrival of a cryptographically-relevant quantum computer.

Cryptography: the study of ensuring the safe transfer and storage of information in an adversarial environment.

Cybersecurity: protecting the organization's information through risk management practices and processes (e.g., prevent, detect, and respond to cybersecurity incidents).

Cybersecurity readiness: the ability of organizations and people to predict and respond to cyber threats and opportunities. Organizations wishing to maintain and improve cybersecurity readiness include continual improvement practices like regular cybersecurity training. A minimum viable cybersecurity foundation that is continually improved is a prerequisite for cybersecurity readiness.

Cybersecurity resilience: the ability of the organization to respond and recover from cybersecurity incidents.

Demand: technology users request existing or new digital products or services, and it is detailed in ITIL's Demand Management practice.

Dual potentialities of technology: technology is inherently neutral; however, it (quantum computing) can be used for good (cure diseases) or bad purposes (steal and decrypt).

Early adopters: individuals and organizations who use new technologies before others (see *Late adopters*).

Encryption: the process of scrambling data so that only the intended parties can unscramble it.

Encryptogeddon: when a cryptographically-relevant quantum computer is used to cause great harm and damage.

Frameworks: represent best practices but usually exist in the absence of well-defined and globally accepted standards. Frameworks are less prescriptive and more flexible than standards.

Guide to the Project Management Body of Knowledge (PMBOK Guide): the ANSI standard for project management representing best practices for most projects, most of the time.

Initiative: a smaller project that requires less governance and supporting documentation. However, project management tools and processes (e.g., risk management) benefit initiatives (see also *Project*).

ISO standards: guides embodying international best practices agreed upon by experts. They often have a certification pathway indicating meeting the required levels of quality to safely deliver the service or product for which they are certified.

ITIL: the Information Technology Infrastructure Library is a service management framework of practices that outline how to plan, deliver, operate, and optimize digital services (see *COBIT*, an alternative framework).

Late adopters: individuals and organizations who use new technologies after others (e.g., after early adopters have stabilized the technology) and are sometimes referred to as laggard adopters (see *Early Adopters*).

Minimum viable foundation: projects and initiatives to achieve thresholds or foundations to build future innovations or leverage intended capabilities; delivering anything less than the minimum foundation (e.g., project, service, change, or cybersecurity management) may result in an unusable product or service.

Mosca's Theorem: a mathematical equation to evaluate an organization's preparedness for the quantum era.

NIST Cybersecurity Framework: the American government's National Institute of Standards and Technology (NIST) provides a cybersecurity approach of best practices to manage cybersecurity risks.

Operations: the phase after project deliverables (e.g., a quantum computer that simulates protein structure predictions in human health and disease research) are provided to the project sponsor who manages the deliverables according to the quantum business case and to the benefit of the organization.

Post-quantum cryptography: cryptographic algorithms that are presumed to be secure from both quantum and classical computer attacks (also known as quantum-safe cryptography and quantum-resistant cryptography; see also *Classical cryptography*).

Progressive elaboration: the iterative process of continuously refining and detailing a project's plans and deliverables as more information becomes available and understanding increases.

Project: a unique and temporary endeavor to create a product or service and the provision of project deliverables to the project sponsor signals project completion (see also *Initiative*).

Project attributes: elements that determine project type including project criticality, complexity, priority, and urgency.

Project criticality: relates to the quantum technology project's importance to achieving the organization's goals and objectives.

Project complexity: a degree of difficulty to plan, manage, and implement a quantum technology project.

Project priority: the project's level of importance to the organization and in relationship with other projects.

Project urgency: how sensitive the timing is to implement quantum technologies—meaning how quickly does the project need to be completed.

Q2K: the challenge of preparing for a cryptographically-relevant quantum computer is compared to the challenges of preparing for Y2K (the year 2000 risk). However, Q2K differs as the risks are clearer, but the date is uncertain.

Q-Day: arrival a cryptographically-relevant quantum computer that can break classical encryption used to keep data and systems secure and requires a transition to quantum-resistance cryptographic systems.

Quantum advantage: a point in time where a quantum computer can solve a problem more efficiently and effectively (e.g., more accurately) than a classical computer irrespective of the solution's utility. Quantum advantage is the preferred term as quantum "supremacy" has negative connotations and is related to racial supremacy for some people.

Quantum business case: provides a high-level or strategic overview of the quantum product or service—developed by the product or service manager—highlighting its alignment with organizational strategy, expected benefits, timelines, costs, return on investment, and associated risks.

Quantum business use case: a detailed or tactical description of how quantum technologies are applied to a specific business problem or opportunity.

Quantum cryptography: applying quantum properties to create cryptographic protocols like quantum key distribution.

Quantum cybersecurity readiness: a state of at least effective post-quantum cryptography and cryptographic agility enabled through continual improvement cycles (projects and initiatives) and built upon a minimum viable cybersecurity foundation.

Quantum key distribution: quantum key distribution (QKD) encrypts and decrypts data with the principles of quantum physics (e.g., superposition and entanglement); however, post-quantum cryptography is generally recommended over QKD.

Quantum readiness: the ability to manage threats related to quantum technologies in the domains of people, processes, and technologies including implementing post-quantum cryptography and developing and maintaining cryptographic agility. Quantum readiness assumes a minimum viable cybersecurity foundation is maintained and continually optimized for both quantum and classical technologies.

Quantum-safe cryptography: the study of cryptographic algorithms that are thought to be secure from both quantum and classical computer attacks (also known as post-quantum cryptography and quantum-resistant cryptography).

Quantum technologies: technologies that apply the principles of quantum physics like quantum computers or quantum sensors.

Quantum vulnerable: a system susceptible to a quantum attack (e.g., the digital ecosystem may have insufficient post-quantum cryptography).

Qubit: the smallest unit of information in quantum computing, like a bit in classical computing, except a qubit can be in both states of 0 and 1 simultaneously (superposition property of quantum mechanics).

Reverse design: design influenced by what is readily available in the supply chain inventory, rather than creating a design and then sourcing the required components, which can introduce supply chain risks of delay.

Risk: an uncertain event or condition that if it occurs results in an issue that can have a positive or negative effect on the project.

Risk tolerance: the amount of risk the organization is willing to accept after a rigorous risk assessment to achieve its vision and objectives.

Risk severity: the probability the risk may occur, multiplied by the impact if the risk occurs.

RSA cryptography: Rivest–Shamir–Adleman (1977) is a public-key encryption algorithm for secure data transmission to encrypt data using two different but linked keys. It is scheduled for deprecation (2030) and disallowance (2035) necessitating the migration to other means like post-quantum cryptography.

Simulation: using quantum technologies including quantum computers to model and simulate physical and chemical systems at the quantum level.

Steal now, decrypt later: to steal data and wait until quantum tools are available to decrypt the data (also known as "record now, exploit later").

Tailor: to bring in and adapt standards, frameworks, techniques, tools, and processes suitable for one's project. In *Quantum Cybersecurity*, we consider tailoring to adapting within the framework, standard, or method and combining to bring in techniques, tools, and processes from other frameworks, standards, or methods.

Technical maturity stack: the degree of organizational capability regarding project management, cybersecurity, technology service management, and organizational change management.

Uncertainty: the degree of unpredictability of some or all project elements (e.g., scope, cost, time, and communications).

Urgency: the importance of completing a project by a certain time often driven by business requirements like meeting external regulatory requirements.

Value: technology users' perception of the benefits of digital products or services, usefulness and importance that are provided by the organization; is central to ITIL's Service Value System and Service Value Chain.

Vision: the aspiration of what the organization will become in the target (future) state.

Workshop: a "hands-on" meeting where participants collaborate to develop (co-create) something of value that allows the project to progress such as a workshop to develop a schedule or a design workshop.

Y2K (Year 2000): called the Millennium Bug, it was a computer glitch that triggered global fears of catastrophic failures in critical systems as the date changed from 1999 to 2000. While Q-Day shares similarities with Y2K, there is a key difference: Y2K required extensive preparation, and it had almost no impact, whereas Q-Day introduces a long-term vulnerability that may or may not be exploited over time.

References

Ali, Muhammad A., Asif Mahmood, Usman Zafar, and Muhammad Nazim. 2021. "The Power of ADKAR Change Model in Innovative Technology, Acceptance under the Moderating Effect of Culture and Open Innovation." *LogForum* 17 (4): 485–502. https://www.google.com/search?q=The+Power+of+ADKAR+Change+Model+in+Innovative+Technology%2C+Acceptance+under+the+Moderating+Effect+of+Culture+and+Open+Innovation&rlz=1C1GCEB_enAU1082AU1082&oq=The+Power+of+ADKAR+Change+Model+in+Innovative+Technology%2C+Acceptance+under+the+Moderating+Effect+of+Culture+and+Open+Innovation&gs_lcrp=EgZjaHJvbWUyBggAEEUYOTIHCAEQIRiPAtIBCDk3MmowajE1qAIIsAIB8QVa64EU2tMjMfEFWuuBFNrTIzE&sourceid=chrome&ie=UTF-8.

Association of Change Management Professionals. 2025. "Standard for Change Management." https://www.acmpglobal.org/page/the_standard.

Austin, Robert B., Pardis Pishdad-Bozorgi, and Jesus M. de la Garza. 2016. "Identifying and Prioritizing Best Practices to Achieve Flash Track Projects." *Journal of Construction Engineering and Management* 142 (2). https://doi.org/10.1061/(ASCE)CO.1943-7862.0001061.

Australian Signals Directorate. 2022. "Essential Eight." https://www.cyber.gov.au/resources-business-and-government/essential-cybersecurity/essential-eight.

AXELOS. 2019. *ITIL Foundation: ITIL 4 Edition.* The Stationery Office Ltd.

AXELOS. 2020. "*Strategy Management: ITIL 4 Practice Guide.*" https://www.axelos.com/resource-hub/practice/strategy-management-itil-4-practice-guide.

Ballesteros-Pérez, Pablo, Kamel Mohamed Elamrousy, and Carmen González-Cruz. 2019. "Non-Linear Time-Cost Trade-Off Models of Activity Crashing: Application to Construction Scheduling and Project Compression with Fast-Tracking." *Automation in Construction* 97: 229–40. https://doi.org/10.1016/j.autcon.2018.11.001.

Bertels, Heidi, M. J., Murad Mithani, Siwei Zhu, and Peter A. Koen. 2020. "Corporate Champions of Early-Stage Project Proposals and Institutionalizations of Organizational Inertia." *International Journal of Innovation Management* 24 (3): 2050028. https://doi.org/10.1142/S1363919620500280.

Bogus, S. M., J. E. Diekmann, K. R. Molenaar, C. Harper, S. Patil, and J. S. Lee. 2011. "Simulation of Overlapping Design Activities in Concurrent Engineering." *Journal of Construction Engineering and Management* 137 (11): 950–7. https://doi.org/10.1061/(ASCE)CO.1943-7862.0000363.

Brooks, Frederick P. 1975. *The Mythical Man-Month: Essays on Software Engineering.* Addison-Wesley Pub. Co.

CFDIR (Canadian Forum for Digital Infrastructure Resilience). 2024. *Canadian National Quantum-Readiness: Best Practices and Guidelines—Version 4,* July 10. https://ised-isde.canada.ca/site/spectrum-management-telecommunications/sites/default/files/documents/Quantum-Readiness%20Best%20Practices%20-%20v04%20-%2010%20July%202024.pdf.

Chen, Ling-Kun, Rui-Peng Yuan, Xing-Jun Ji, et al. 2021. "Modular Composite Building in Urgent Emergency Engineering Projects: A Case Study of Accelerated Design and Construction of Wuhan Thunder God Mountain/Leishenshan Hospital to COVID-19 Pandemic." *Automation in Construction* 124: 103555. https://doi.org/10.1016/j.autcon.2021.103555.

CISA (Cybersecurity and Infrastructure Security Agency). 2023. "Cybersecurity Performance Goals." https://www.cisa.gov/cross-sector-cybersecurity-performance-goals.

Davis, Fred D. 1989. "Perceived Usefulness, Perceived Ease of Use, and User Acceptance of Information Technology." *MIS Quarterly* 13 (3): 319–40. https://doi.org/10.2307/249008.

Da Veiga, Adéle. 2018. "An Approach to Information Security Culture Change Combining ADKAR and the ISCA Questionnaire to Aid Transition to the Desired Culture." *Information and Computer Security* 26 (5): 584–612. https://doi.org/10.1108/ICS-08-2017-0056.

Department of Industry, Science and Resources. 2023. *National Quantum Strategy.* Australian Government. https://www.industry.gov.au/sites/default/files/2023-05/national-quantum-strategy.pdf. Defense Contract Management Agency. 2005. "14-Point Schedule Assessment." https://www.dcma.mil/WBT/dsm/.

Feynman, Richard P. (1982). "Simulating Physics with Computers." *International Journal of Theoretical Physics* 21 (6–7): 467–88. https://doi.org/10.1007/BF02650179.

Fisher, Roger, William Ury, and Bruce Patton. 1999. *Getting to Yes: Negotiating an Agreement Without Giving In.* Completely revised 2nd ed. Random House Business Books.

Government of Canada. 2022. "Canada's National Quantum Strategy." https://ised-isde.canada.ca/site/national-quantum-strategy/sites/default/files/attachments/2022/NQS-SQN-eng.pdf.

Howell, Jane M. 2005. "The Right Stuff: Identifying and Developing Effective Champions of Innovation." *Academy of Management Perspectives* 19 (2): 108–19. https://doi.org/10.5465/AME.2005.16965104.

Hubbart, J. A. 2023. "Organizational Change: Considering Truth and Buy-In." *Administrative Sciences* 13 (1): 1–8. https://doi.org/10.3390/admsci13010003.

Kanter, Rosabeth M. 1983. *The Change Masters: Innovation for Productivity in the American Corporation*. Simon & Schuster.

Kelley, Donna, and Hyunsuk Lee. 2010. "Managing Innovation Champions: The Impact of Project Characteristics on the Direct Manager Role." *The Journal of Product Innovation Management* 27 (7): 1007–19. https://doi .org/10.1111/j.1540-5885.2010.00767.x.

Kerzner, Harold. 2013. *Project Management a Systems Approach to Planning, Scheduling, and Controlling*. 11th ed. John Wiley & Sons, Inc. https://www.wiley .com/en-au/Project+Management%3A+A+Systems+Approach+to+ Planning%2C+Scheduling%2C+and+Controlling%2C+11th+Edition -p-9781118415856.

Lu, Hui, Hongwei Wang, Dihua Yu, and Jian Ye. 2023. "Sharp Schedule Compression in Urgent Emergency Construction Projects via Activity Crashing, Substitution and Overlapping: A Case Study of Huoshenshan and Leishenshan Hospital Projects in Wuhan." *Engineering, Construction, and Architectural Management* 30 (8): 3696–3712. https://doi.org/10.1108 /ECAM-07-2021-0654.

Ma, Chujiao, Luis Colon, Joe Dera, Bahman Rashidi, and Vaibhav Garg. 2021. "CARAF: Crypto Agility Risk Assessment Framework." *Journal of Cybersecurity* 7 (1): tyab013. https://doi.org/10.1093/cybsec/tyab013.

Maraqa, Saf'a N., Deniz Berfin Karakoc, Nafiseh Ghorbani-Renani, Kash Barker, and Andrés D González. 2022. "Project Schedule Compression for the Efficient Restoration of Interdependent Infrastructure Systems." *Computers & Industrial Engineering* 170: 108342. https://doi.org/10.1016/j.cie.2022 .108342.

Martins, Claudia Garrido, Susan M. Bogus, and Vanessa Valentin. 2023. "Quantitative Risk Assessment Model and Optimization in Infrastructure Fast-Track Construction Projects." *Infrastructures (Basel)* 8 (4): 78. https://doi .org/10.3390/infrastructures8040078.

Mosca, Michele, and Marco Piani. 2024. "Quantum Threat Timeline Report 2024." *Global Risk Institute*. https://globalriskinstitute.org /publication/2024-quantum-threat-timeline-report/.

NIST. 2020. "NIST IR 8286: Integrating Cybersecurity and Enterprise Risk Management (ERM)." https://csrc.nist.gov/pubs/ir/8286/final.

NIST. 2021. "Getting Ready for Post-Quantum Cryptography: Exploring Challenges Associated with Adopting and Using Post-Quantum Cryptographic Algorithms." https://csrc.nist.gov/pubs/cswp/15/getting-ready-for -postquantum-cryptography/final.

NIST. 2024a. *Cybersecurity Framework (CSF) 2.0*. https://www.nist.gov /cyberframework.

NIST. 2024b. "NIST IR 8547 (Initial Public Draft)." *Transition to Post-Quantum Cryptography Standards*. https://csrc.nist.gov/pubs/ir/8547/ipd.

NSW Government. 2024. "Transport for New South Wales: Quantum Technology." https://www.transport.nsw.gov.au/system/files/media/documents/2021 /Transport%20for%20NSW%20and%20Quantum%20Technology%20-% 20WCAG%20version.PDF.

Pádár, Katalin, Béla Pataki, and Zoltán Sebestyén. 2017. "Bringing Project and Change Management Roles into Sync." *Journal of Organizational Change Management* 30 (4): 495–510. https://doi.org/10.1108/JOCM-07-2016-0128.

Parlakkiliç, A., and N. Ünalan. 2021. "Assessment of Health Information System Change Resistance." *Academic Journal of Information Technology* 12 (44): 37–46. https://doi.org/10.5824/ajite.2021.01.003.x.

Perryman, Aaron, Alexey Bocharnikov, Charles Lim, and Kaushik Chakraborty. 2024. *Improving Tomorrow's Security by Decoding the Quantum Computing Threat.* https://www.ey.com/en_au/cybersecurity/improving-tomorrow-s -security-by-decoding-the-quantum-computing-threat

Project Management Institute. 2017a. *A Guide to the Project Management Body of Knowledge: PMBOK Guide.* 6th ed. Project Management Institute, Inc.

Project Management Institute. 2017b. *The Standard for Program Management.* 4th ed. Project Management Institute.

Project Management Institute. 2017c. *Agile Practice Guide.* Project Management Institute.

Rasul, Nazia, Muhammad Sohail Anwar Malik, Beenish Bakhtawar, and Muhammad Jamaluddin Thaheem. 2021. "Risk Assessment of Fast-Track Projects: A Systems-Based Approach." *International Journal of Construction Management* 21 (11): 1099–114. https://doi.org/10.1080/15623599.2019. 1602587.

Salhab, Diana, Søren Munch Lindhard, and Farook Hamzeh. 2023. "Schedule Compression and Emerging Waste in Construction: An Assessment of Overlapping Activities." *Engineering, Construction, and Architectural Management* 31 (12): 4920–41. https://doi.org/10.1108/ECAM-12-2022-1121.

Schon, D. A. 1963. "Champions for Radical New Inventions." *Harvard Business Review* 41 (2). Harvard University Graduate School of Business Administration. https://www.scienceopen.com /document?vid=7a5ede36-a993-4268-b523-4f4b5f0a3606

Schwaber, Ken, and Jeff Sutherland. 2020. "The Scrum Guide™." *Scrum Guides.* https://scrumguides.org/.

Skulmoski, Greg. 2022. *Shields Up: Cybersecurity Project Management.* Business Expert Press.

Skulmoski, Greg, and Francis Hartman. 2000. "The Project's Achilles Heel: Misalignment." *Cost Engineering* 42 (12). https://www.proquest.com /docview/220443814?_oafollow=false&accountid=26503&pq-origsite= primo&sourcetype=Scholarly%20Journals

Skulmoski Greg, and Francis Hartman. 2010. "Information Systems Project Manager Soft Competencies: A Project-Phase Investigation." *Project Management Journal* 41 (1): 61–80. https://doi.org/10.1002/pmj.20146.

Skulmoski, Greg, and Ashkan Memari. 2025a. *Quantum Cybersecurity Program Management.* Business Expert Press.

Skulmoski, Greg, and Ashkan Memari. 2025b. "Get Ready for the Next Generation of AI Quantum Technologies." In *Voices of Innovation-AI*, edited by Ed Marx. HIMSS Book Series, Taylor & Francis Group.

Skulmoski, Greg, and Chris Walker. 2023. *Cybersecurity Training: A Pathway to Readiness.* Business Expert Press.

Tan, Tan, Grant Mills, Jiqiang Hu, and Eleni Papadonikolaki. 2021. "Integrated Approaches to Design for Manufacture and Assembly: A Case Study of Huoshenshan Hospital to Combat COVID-19 in Wuhan, China." *Journal of Management in Engineering* 37 (6). https://doi.org/10.1061/(ASCE)ME.1943-5479.0000972.

Tomczak, Michal, and Piotr Jaskowski. 2020. "Crashing Construction Project Schedules by Relocating Resources." *IEEE Access* 8: 224522–31. https://doi.org/10.1109/ACCESS.2020.3044645.

Turkoglu, Harun, Gul Polat, and Firat Dogu Akin. 2023. "Crashing Construction Projects Considering Schedule Flexibility: An Illustrative Example." *International Journal of Construction Management* 23 (4): 619–28. https://doi.org/10.1080/15623599.2021.1901559.

van Laere, Joeri, and Lena Aggestam. 2016. "Understanding Champion Behaviour in a Health-Care Information System Development Project— How Multiple Champions and Champion Behaviours Build a Coherent Whole." *European Journal of Information Systems* 25 (1): 47–63. https://doi.org/10.1057/ejis.2015.5.

Venkatesh, Viswanath, and Fred. D. Davis. 2000. "A Theoretical Extension of the Technology Acceptance Model: Four longitudinal field studies." *Management Science* 46 (2): 186–204. https://doi.org/10.1287/mnsc.46.2.186.11926.

Winter, Ron. 2011. "DCMA-14 Point Schedule Assessment." https://www.ronwinterconsulting.com/DCMA_14-Point_Assessment.pdf.

World Economic Forum. 2022. "Transitioning to a Quantum-Secure Economy." https://www3.weforum.org/docs/WEF_Transitioning%20to_a_Quantum_Secure_Economy_2022.pdf.

World Economic Forum. 2024. "Quantum for Society: Meeting the Ambition of the SDGs." https://www.weforum.org/publications/quantum-for-society-fulfilling-the-promise-of-the-sdgs/.

Young, R., and E. Jordan. 2008. "Top Management Support: Mantra or Necessity?" *International Journal of Project Management* 26 (7): 713–25. https://doi.org/10.1016/j.ijproman.2008.06.001.

Author Biography

Gregory J. Skulmoski has had two career paths: as an academic who leads the Project Innovation Management graduate program at Bond University, and as a technology project manager. Greg has led pioneering technology projects, including cybersecurity, IoT, Lean Six Sigma process improvement, and auditing/compliance projects. Greg used the tools and processes described in *Quantum Cybersecurity Program Management* to win the 2017 Middle East Security Award, and was recognized by the CISO Council (Chief Information Security Officer Council) as one of the 100 Rising Stars in Security and Risk (for risk management in technology projects).

Greg was a core member of the PMBOK Guide 2000 Update Team that revised the original PMI PMBOK Guide. He is honored to have contributed to other standards such as PMI's Practice Standard for Work Breakdown Structures, Organizational Project Management Maturity Model, and Project Manager Competency Development Framework. Greg participated and contributed to the NIST Cybersecurity Framework (CSF) v2.0 update project and other global and domestic cybersecurity initiatives. Dr. Skulmoski is a Certified Information Technology Professional and a lifelong Fellow of the British Computer Society.

Therefore, Greg Skulmoski brings both practical experience and a broad theoretical background in project management and cybersecurity, leading to his lean approach to cybersecurity project management. Greg is the author of *Shields Up: Cybersecurity Project Management* (2022), *Cybersecurity Training: A Pathway to Readiness* (2023) with Chris Walker, and the Amazon Top New Release (January 2025) *Quantum Cybersecurity*

Program Management with Dr. Ashkan Memari published by Business Expert Press debuting as Amazon's Top New Release. Greg was part of the Tasmanian Quantum Network team that won the 2025 International Quantum Strategy Day international competition sponsored by the Quantum Strategy Institute, where they applied the concepts from his books to support the winning quantum strategy.

Greg Skulmoski won the Australian Institute of Project Management 2025 Project Management Achievement Award for Research for his four books about cybersecurity and quantum technologies project management; "This award-winning research advanced the discipline of project management through rigorous methodology, insight, and practical relevance" (award commendation).

Other Books by Greg Skulmoski

Greg Skulmoski has written a series of books about emerging technologies project management including cybersecurity, artificial intelligence, and quantum technologies. These books were positively reviewed by leading experts and are critically acclaimed. Thank you!

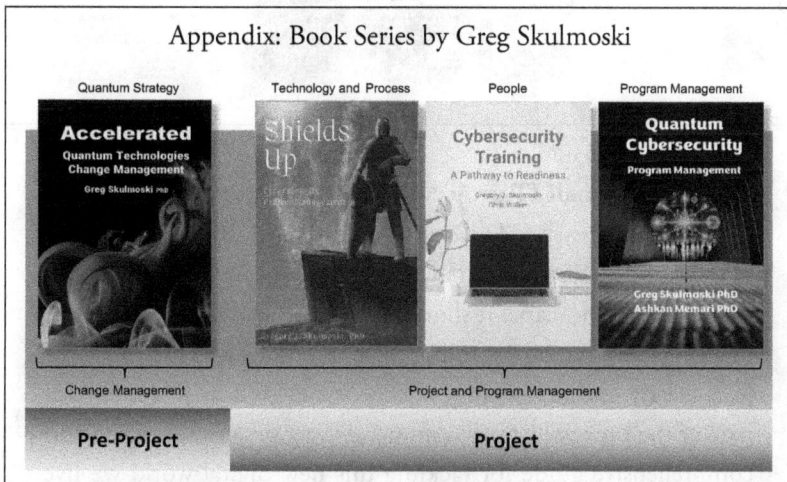

Appendix: Book Series by Greg Skulmoski

Shields Up: Cybersecurity Project Management

Shields Up: Cybersecurity Project Management explains how to effectively plan, manage, and deliver technology and cybersecurity projects. The book provides a framework that incorporates best practices from various disciplines, including project management, risk management, quality management, and technology service management. The book is intended for both experienced cybersecurity professionals and those new to the field who are taking on project leadership roles.

Appendix: *Shields Up: Cybersecurity Project Management*

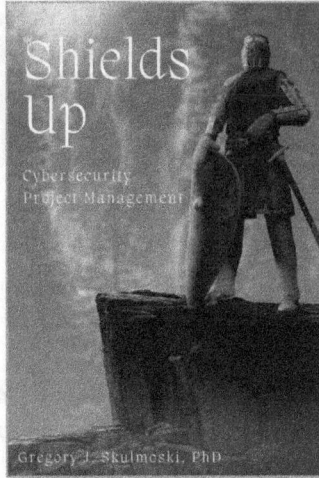

"Must-read for all IT project managers"
Cybersecurity Project Management (Skulmoski 2022) is comprehensive and incredibly timely, given the ever-increasing cybersecurity threat landscape. It should be a must-read for all IT project managers because of the importance of ensuring that all IT projects clearly and deliberately address cyber risks as just a normal part of the process. I must commend Greg on a well-written and comprehensive guide for tackling this new digital world we live in. Well done!

Jason Roos, Chief Information Officer, King Abdullah
University of Science and Technology, Saudi Arabia

"Best I have seen in my career"
You say many useful things about project management that I value and know. Some of your explanations of familiar topics and tools are among the best I have seen in my career.

Distinguished Professor Emeritus Timothy Kloppenborg, PhD,
Project Management, Xavier University, United States

Cybersecurity Training: A Pathway to Readiness

Cybersecurity Training: A Pathway to Readiness is a comprehensive guide to develop effective cybersecurity training programs within organizations. The authors provide a project-oriented approach based on industry-standard frameworks like ITIL, NIST, and ISO, as well as proven training best practices such as ADDIE Model of Instructional Design, Bloom's Taxonomy of Cognitive Thought, and Kirkpatrick's Model of Evaluation.

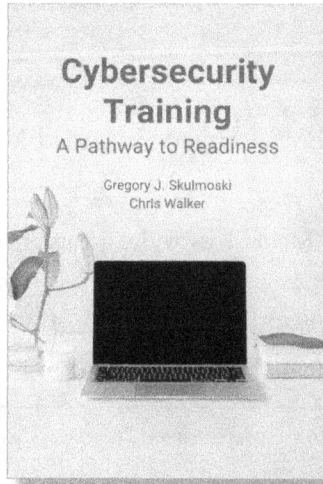

Appendix: *Cybersecurity Training: A Pathway to Readiness*

"An incredible book that empowered and inspired me"

Cybersecurity Training is an incredible book that empowered and inspired me. The authors, Greg and Chris, write with a genuine passion for cybersecurity readiness and its critical role in the success and survival of organizations. Overall, *Cybersecurity Training* is an incredible book that empowered and inspired me to act and make a difference in the fight against cyber threats.

Charles Aunger, CEO/President/Founder,

HEAL Security Inc., USA

"The first worldwide reference"

As a business analyst, program manager, and professional trainer for over 20 years, I have found *Cybersecurity Training* as the first worldwide reference combining cybersecurity, project management and training with a ready-to-action perspective. Read it, study it, and tailor it to your specific context. Get ready now to help your organization proactively manage cybersecurity risks.

Rafa Pagán, MSc, CBAP, CPOA, AAC, PMP, PMI-ACP, PMI-PBA, PMI-RMP, PMI-SP, OPEN PM2, KANBAN, POWER BI, MCTS, MCITP, CTT+, SAMC, SDC, SMC, SPOC, SSMC, SSPOC, CSM, CSPO, PSM, PSPO, COMPTIA

Quantum Cybersecurity Program Management

Quantum Cybersecurity Program Management, written by Gregory J. Skulmoski and Ashkan Memari, provides a comprehensive guide for organizations transitioning to a secure quantum ecosystem. It was Amazon's Top New Release on January 7, 2025.

Appendix: *Quantum Cybersecurity Program Management*

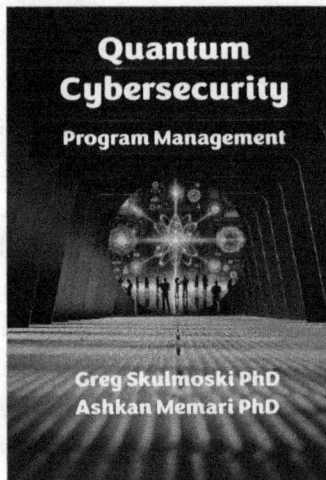

"Quantum readiness expertly simplified and decoded"

I have read many books and documents about quantum technologies having authored *Quantum Nation: India's Leap into the Future,* but none have clearly laid out a practical pathway to quantum readiness. I really like this book.

L. Venkata Subramaniam, PhD (Indian Institute of Technology Delhi, India), IBM Quantum India Lead, IBM Master Inventor

"Indispensable guide to quantum technology project"

Quantum Cybersecurity Program Management is a seminal work that masterfully addresses the imminent challenges posed by quantum technologies to modern cybersecurity frameworks. This is essential reading for C-level executives, IT professionals, cybersecurity experts, and, especially, project managers, who will find invaluable guidance for navigating the complexities of quantum project management.

Julio Bandeira de Melo, Cybersecurity Leader, Canada

"I highly recommend it to all technology leaders and project managers"

Quantum Cybersecurity Program Management gives actionable steps for project managers, IT managers, and executives alike. By aligning with multiple standards and best practices, it ensures that readers can easily incorporate lessons learned into their current work practices and business strategies. It is a great read, and I highly recommend it to all technology leaders and project managers.

Jake McGaffin, MBA, MEM, CSM, Project Manager, Gensco Inc., United States

Index

www.ingramcontent.com/pod-product-compliance
Lightning Source LLC
Chambersburg PA
CBHW061209220326
41599CB00025B/4579